A City in Racial Crisis

Leonard Gordon

A City
in Racial Crisis

A City
in Racial Crisis

The Case of Detroit Pre- and Post- the 1967 Riot

Leonard Gordon
Arizona State University

WM. C. BROWN COMPANY PUBLISHERS

Copyright © 1971 by
Wm. C. Brown Company Publishers

ISBN 0-697-07576-1

Library of Congress Catalog Card Number:
72-133622.

Printed in the United States of America

To the Future:

Sue, Matt, Melissa
and
Rena

contents

3 The Post-Riot Period

maps and tables
Detroit metropolitan data

foreword

The urban racial conflict is the central crisis facing American society today and in the foreseeable future. Presented in this book are articles, based on extensive research, which encompass all the variables of this crisis.

Detroit until 1967 was reputed to be perhaps the most progressive city in terms of interracial cooperation and planning. But these promises, hopes and plans of equal opportunity and full justice were never, in fact, realized. These unfulfilled promises set the stage for the greatest urban disruption in American history. This book is important because it analyzes what went wrong and catalogs new attempts that may close the racial gap.

Dr. Gordon, in a masterful way, has brought the skills of social scientists to bear in assessing the possible future directions for Detroit, and by implication, for all our cities. This is a pragmatic analysis of the options that are still open for interracial accommodation or conflict. At issue is the survival of the American city and democracy itself.

JOHN CONYERS, JR.

Member of Congress
1st District, Michigan

preface

This reader attempts a community-wide perspective on the urban racial crisis confronting our society by providing establishment and disestablishment views and analyses from one city, Detroit, where the most damaging riot in American urban history in lives lost and property damaged occurred in 1967.[1] The Kerner Commission report documented that the community factors which underlie the racial cleavage in Detroit are markedly similar to those operating in Philadelphia (Kensington riot of 1964), Los Angeles (Watts riot of 1965), Cleveland (Hough riot of 1966), and other urban centers.

One recurring explanatory concept is that of the built-in conflict over expectations and reality. In this view the concern is with the social gap between legally guaranteed rights and opportunities such as those embodied in the Economic Opportunity Act of 1965, and the continuing lack of substantial change in the living circumstances and opportunities for the mass of blacks living in inner-city ghettos.[2] Yet, ghettos and inner-city poverty are not new to Detroit or to any other large city. They are a traditional characteristic of the American metropolis. As Robert Park observed in the foreword to Louis Wirth's *The Ghetto,* so many inner-city ethnic and racial groupings have historically been evident in any major American urban setting that "ghettos" can be viewed as "natural areas" of the city.[3] At the time Park and Wirth were writing in the 1920s and earlier, the peoples of these "natural areas"—Italians, Jews, Poles, Greeks, Russians, and other immigrant groups—were often in as poor and in as difficult circumstances as are inner-city blacks. A question often asked is why these early relatively disadvantaged groups generally did not riot. Two of the dynamic factors that make

1. See: *Report of the National Advisory Commission on Civil Disorders,* The Kerner Commission (New York: Bantam Books, Inc., 1968), pp. 115-116, 358, and 611-659.
2. "Conditions of Life in the Racial Ghetto," ibid., pp. 266-277.
3. Robert E. Park, foreword to *The Ghetto,* by Louis Wirth (Chicago: The University of Chicago Press, 1928), p. vi.

the present racial ghettos different and help explain why the inhabitants respond differently are that of race and a changing economic structure. Historical American race prejudice and visibility operate to delimit black movement. As Mack observes about race independent of other socioeconomic characteristics, "the category Negro is invariably relevant in America."[4] An additional complicating factor, as Ferman observes, is related to the changing economic structure in its relation to the unskilled who enter the urban setting. These people often become "displaced workers" victimized by technological change, who cannot find new roles in the labor market.[5] Detroit embodies these factors of race and economics.*

This reader presents analyses and views from a variety of perspectives in one city with the aim of gaining insight into these dynamic forces and others that affect race relations. The focus of the articles is twofold. One is a grass-roots focus dealing with attitudes and residential living patterns. The other is on leadership in Detroit as it has responded and is responding to interracial antipathy. In selecting this latter focus I am using the concept of leadership in its broadest sense. Community leadership—as in Merton's classic analysis of influentials in Rovere[6]—generally takes into consideration particular economic, social, and political "influentials" who as individuals can and do influence substantial numbers of other community members on issues of general community concern. This traditional view of leadership appears to be too narrow to be valid for Detroit or for any contemporary urban community. Urban leadership is a complex mosaic of corporate executives, union officials, officeholders, educators, religious spokesmen, and others. And the Detroit experience points up an additional leadership factor, namely, that the ghetto masses spawn a variety of leadership types that respond assertively to their disadvantaged community circumstances. This leadership's actions, combined with the severe relative deprivation of social and economic conditions in the inner city, result in in-

---

*Although it is beyond the scope here, it is useful to note that the lack of acceptance of minority status is related to the demise of the colonial concept and to the emergence of a coequal self-identity of nonwhite minority peoples symbolized by the "black is beautiful" and "Afro-American" movements. See: Stokely Carmichael and Charles Hamilton, *Black Power* (New York: Random House, Inc., 1967); Frantz Fanon, *The Wretched of the Earth: A Negro Psychoanalyst's Study of the Problems of Racism and Colonialism in the World Today* (New York: Grove Press, Inc., 1966); and James W. Vander Zanden, "Minority Reactions to Dominance," Part IV in *American Minority Relations* (New York: The Ronald Press, 1966), pp. 337-445.

4. Raymond W. Mack, *Race, Class and Power*, 2nd ed. (New York: American Book Company, 1968), p. 343.

5. Louis Ferman, with Joyce Kornbluh and Alan Haber, *Poverty in America* (Ann Arbor: The University of Michigan Press, 1965), p. xv.

6. Robert K. Merton, "Patterns of Influence: Local and Cosmopolitan Influentials," in *Social Theory and Social Structure*, 2nd ed. (Glencoe, Illinois: The Free Press, 1959), pp. 387-420.

ducing overt responses from establishment leadership. Thus, the selections make clear that although the riot of 1967 was not planned or organized, those who did riot were influenced by the articulated views of black nationalist leaders such as Malcolm X and his local supporters, and in turn this influence drew major responses from business leader Joseph L. Hudson, Jr., and his peers in the Detroit establishment. The complexity of the social division within this conflict context is evident by noting that Detroit business and labor leadership was of an accommodating nature, while simultaneously the general white suburban reaction was of a volatively negative nature.

The articles document these countervailing social forces operating in Detroit. They are divided into three time periods covering the decade of the 1960s. The 1967 racial disorders represent the pivotal period with articles relating to the pre-riot and post-riot periods. Encompassed are the end of the cohesive Civil Rights Movement and the shift to direct confrontation and conflict. While the articles fall into discrete time periods pre- and post-1967, there is considerable overlap of events in them. This is the result of most of the articles, including two in the first part, having been written from the perspective of the post-riot period. I believe that coupled with earlier dated material this is an advantage, as a more comprehensive analysis is provided by noting the interaction of social responses before, during, and following the riot period. The relation of the particular responses in Detroit to the generic urban-racial crisis in American society is evident in a review of the index. In it are included many indigenous Detroit leadership—for example, Rev. Albert B. Cleage, Jr., and Joseph L. Hudson, Jr.—and Detroit organizations—such as the West Central Organization and the Commission on Community Relations, originally an outgrowth of the 1943 Detroit Race Riot. In the index are also included national leadership—two are Saul Alinsky and Malcolm X— and national organizations—for example, the Congress of Racial Equality and the National Association for the Advancement of Colored People—whose influence was and is felt in Detroit.

The first article is by two former professors of sociology at Wayne State University, located in midtown Detroit. Albert J. Mayer and Thomas F. Hoult provided a clear documentation of the growing ecological and social distance between blacks and whites in Detroit. This was at a time in the early 1960s when it was generally assumed by both supporters and opponents that residential integration was advancing. In fact it was receding. Hoult's follow-up commentary, written five years after the joint effort with Mayer, is from the perspective of one who regretfully confirms his earlier racial conflict diagnosis. The last article is also by a Wayne State professor of sociology with considerable political experience. Mel Ravitz has been an elected Councilman in Detroit since 1962, spanning the pre- and post-riot periods. His perspective is, appropriately, both analytical and social action-oriented. The articles between these are from a variety of perspectives. Those by Charles W. Butler, Malcolm X, Robert A. Mendelsohn, and one from the *Detroit Scope Magazine* offer a view of the militantly discontented inner-city blacks. Those by former mayor Jerome P. Cavanagh, Thomas R. Forrest, Donald Lief, Richard V. Marks, Donald I. Warren, and myself offer a view of the social, economic, and political establishment responses in Detroit. The two articles on the religious establishment, one by Forrest and one by myself, are designed to provide a view of the one institutional leadership that prior to, during, and subsequent to the 1967 rioting crisis attempted to serve in a catalytic role between the discontented inner-city blacks and the overtly contented outer-city whites. The selection on the Detroit riot from the "Report of the National Advisory Commission on Civil Disorders" is included as a well-documented account of the social results of the unresolved conflicting social forces yet operating in Detroit around the issue of race.

acknowledgments

Helpful suggestions were made by a number of people in developing this reader. I particularly want to acknowledge those of fellow Arizona State University faculty—William Anderson, Thomas Hoult, John Hudson, Albert Mayer, and Kimball Young—and former Wayne State University associates—Russell Bright, Abraham Citron, Louis Ferman, and Mel Ravitz. My successor as Michigan Area Director of the American Jewish Committee, Sherwood Sandweiss, provided a stream of most useful materials and views as did former associates working with the Metropolitan Detroit Religion and Race Conference and Interfaith Emergency Council, including Rev. James Bristah, Rev. John Forsyth, Mildred Jefferies, Arthur Johnson, Rev. Hubert Locke, David Roth, Father James Sheehan, Stanley Webb, and Rev. Woody White.

A faculty research grant from Arizona State University for 1968-1969 was a considerable asset.

Edward Cooney, editor, and Ruth Richard, assistant production editor, have my sincere thanks for their highly professional assistance in seeing this manuscript through to final publication.

My wife Rena supplied insightful proofreading and, as in everything, support all the way.

The Pre-Riot Period

The first three articles in part one are analytic. Mayer and Hoult accurately documented the growing ecological and social disparity between the races in Detroit. They did this five years before the destructive riots of 1967. As Hoult notes in his post-riot commentary, this early accurate diagnosis resulted more in an attack on the prognosticators than on the issues raised by the prognosis. The Mayer and Hoult analyses point up the reality that pervasive racial segregation, which came to society-wide attention after the 1954 *Brown* desegregation decision, is not a uniquely Southern or educational phenomenon. Gordon provides an historical account of the one area of institutional establishment leadership—the organized religious community—that attempted to arouse the conscience of the white community to its overt hostility and apathy in the face of deteriorating economic, educational, and social conditions for Detroit's black residents vis-à-vis the white community. The account is one of fundamental ineffectiveness prior to the riot. Yet, the cooperative interreligious efforts of the early and mid sixties layed the groundwork for these institutional leaders to serve in a catalytic role between the varying inner-city black and outer-city white communities during and following the disorders.

The latter four articles, or "messages" as they are entitled in part one, are more in the form of social advocacy than analysis. The first three are based upon speeches given at the interreligiously sponsored city-wide Open Occupancy Conference held January 2 and 3, 1963, at the University of Michigan Rackham Memorial in Detroit. These speeches are by two establishment white leaders and one establishment black leader. The white leaders, Mayor Jerome Cavanagh and Richard Marks, while perceptive of the racial divisions, were hopeful and apparently believed that progress was keeping pace with the specific problems of white racism and the continuing lack of socioeconomic opportunities for most blacks. Their focus, as was the conference's, was on middle- and upper-middle-class Negroes in Detroit rather than upon the ghetto masses. As Mr. Marks, then Executive Director of the Detroit Commission on Community Relations, observed in his address, "To our (Detroit's) eternal credit we have learned from our errors of the past." This was a direct reference to the apparent progress Detroit had made since the 1943 race riot which resulted in the creation of the commission. A less sanguine view was presented by the black minister Charles Butler. Mr. Butler concluded that the black "rebellion is proof-positive that the Negro has grown weary of being the eternal afterthought of America."

If the black and white representatives appeared to be talking past each other in the same conference setting, the larger issue of interracial communication breakdown and black alienation is evident by reviewing Malcolm X's "Message to the Grass Roots." The article by Malcolm X is based upon a talk he gave at a closed black nationalist meeting of the Detroit-based Group on Advanced Leadership (GOAL) early in November, 1963. In it he perceived racism as transcending the democratic-totalitarian or capitalistic-communistic ideological conflicts. The Soviet Union and the United States are both viewed as racist white-dominated societies, whereas democratic and authoritarian regimes in Africa and Asia are viewed as combating white racism. To listen to the recording of the speech made by the Afro-American Broadcasting and Recording Company in Detroit is to gain insight into Malcolm X's appeal and rapport with his supporters in the black ghetto. The speech was given days before President Kennedy's assassination and Malcolm X's severance from the Black Muslims. Represented here is an important perspective of many black ghetto residents.

It is noteworthy that included in the leadership of GOAL, the group that sponsored Malcolm X, is the Reverend Albert B. Cleage, Jr. Mr. Cleage took on this role after resigning from the Detroit Council for Human Rights (DCHR) when the council's chairman, Rev. C. L. Franklin, sought to exclude black nationalists and Freedom Now Party advocates from a pending DCHR conference. Mr. Cleage then initiated with GOAL the conference that featured Malcolm X, while Congressman Adam Clayton Powell spoke to the DCHR.[1] Mr. Cleage was to serve several years later as one of the leading organizers of the National Black Economic Development Conference (NBEDC) held in Detroit, April 25-27, 1969. It was at this NBEDC meeting that James Forman, International Affairs Director of the Student Non-Violent Coordinating Committee, introduced the controversial $500 million black reparations demand in the "Manifesto to the White Christian Churches and Synagogues in the U.S.A. and All Other Racist Institutions." [2] Later in 1969 Mr. Cleage ran unsuccessfully for the presidency of the National Council of Churches and participated in the successful effort to return Robert Williams to the United States after several years' exile in Africa. As the Detroit riot has meaning for the entire society, the implications of this move extends beyond Detroit. Mr. Williams, a former NAACP official in North Carolina, was the first significant black leader to attempt to legitimize the use of violent self-defense as one of the techniques in direct social action.[3]

The content of the articles in part one denotes several community variables that resulted in a socially combustible interracial situation. The factor of a growing ecological separation of blacks and whites is mirrored in the factor of the communication and perspective gaps evident in the statements and positions of communal leadership in each community. A third communal factor in this context was the ineffectual alleviation efforts symbolized by the activities of the Religion and Race Conference. The effect of these efforts tended to intensify the increasing black expectations without achieving major concomitant changes in the status quo. Thus on the eve of the 1967 riot, old racial tensions, which were evident in the 1940s when another major riot occurred[4] and in the 1950s when a Wayne State University study demonstrated that Detroiters viewed race relations as a problem second only to housing,[5] had continued unabated.

1. George Breitman, ed., *Malcolm X Speaks: Selected Speeches and Statements* (New York: Merit Publishers, 1965), pp. 3-4.
2. *The New York Times*, May 7, 1969.
3. Inge Powell Bell, "Legitimation of Self-Defense: Robert Williams," in Bell, *CORE and the Strategy of Non-Violence* (New York: Random House, Inc., 1968), pp. 53-57. For a detailed account of Mr. Cleage's social outlook and specific support of Malcolm X see: Albert B. Cleage, Jr., "Brother Malcolm," in Cleage, *The Black Messiah* (New York: Sheed and Ward, 1968), pp. 186-200.
4. Alfred M. Lee and Norman D. Humphrey, *Race Riot* (New York: Holt, Rinehart and Winston, 1943).
5. Arthur Kornhauser, *Attitudes of Detroit People Toward Detroit* (Detroit: Wayne University Press, 1952), p. 25

Race and Residence
in Detroit

Albert J. Mayer and Thomas F. Hoult

Negro Detroiters are more segregated in their housing today than they were three decades ago.

Available data prove this point beyond question, although the statement itself may seem surprising to those who have witnessed the "invasion" of one "white" neighborhood after another. The statement is also at variance with our democratic pretensions. "Fair housing for all," we proclaim. But the housing used by Negro citizens is almost entirely what is best described as *Ghettoized.*

If this is true, some will ask, how can we explain the existence of so many neighborhoods which were once occupied solely by Caucasians but which now have one or more Negro families? What about the whispering campaigns—"Mr. X is showing his house to 'anyone' "? What about those calls from real estate agents?—"Your neighborhood is next. Better sell before the panic." And what about the "Improvement Associations"? Such phenomena suggest a widespread move toward (as well as resistance to) housing integration.

But, to date, *there is no such move.* The apparent discrepancy is explained by this simple fact: As Detroit's Negro population has increased it has spilled out to occupy housing available in adjacent areas. And, since the increase has been constant (due to an excess of births over deaths and to a high in-migration rate), the "spilling" process has been constant. Thus, many Caucasian neighborhoods have been "invaded," giving rise to the idea that those who believe in integrated housing were being fulfilled at last.

But what has actually occurred is that the specific position only, not the existence or the relative location of what may be termed the "Black Ghetto"

The authors, presently at Arizona State University, were Director and Associate Director, respectively, of the Wayne State University Institute of Regional and Urban Studies in Detroit at the time this analysis was originally written in 1962. Reprinted by permission.

walls has been altered by internal pressure. In addition, the wall has become increasingly impenetrable. These central facts are dramatically demonstrated by the accompanying tables and maps which show that—

a. Detroit's Negro population remains concentrated in segregated areas;
b. the distance between the center line of Negro and the center line of white population is constantly greater;
c. a constantly decreasing number of Negroes live in areas populated by a significant number of whites; and,
d. all but an insignificant number of Detroit area census tracts have remained racially unchanged *or* have become increasingly ghettoized as Negro housing districts.

Maps 1 through 4, based on census data, depict the location of the Detroit area's major and minor Negro "ghettos" from 1930 through 1960. The most notable feature of these maps is their clear demonstration that Negroes in the 1960 decade live in essentially the same places that their predecessors lived during the 1930's—the only difference is that, due to increasing numbers, they occupy more space *centered about their traditional quarters.*

The fact that the Detroit area Negro population remains as concentrated as ever is depicted in still another way by Maps 5 through 9. These maps show what may be termed the center line of population concentration for each racial group in 1940, 1950 and 1960.[1] On Map 5, the center line of white population is shown to have moved steadily outward on almost all sides, thus reflecting the well-known flight of whites toward the suburbs. In contrast, the center line of Negro population, shown on Map 6, has actually moved inward, a movement which reflects the relatively great increase in the number of Negroes concentrated in the older areas of Detroit. Maps 7, 8 and 9 compare the center lines of the two racial groups in three census years. In 1940 (Map 7), the center lines intersected one another in such a way as to suggest a considerable amount of integrated housing. By 1950 (Map 8), the center lines were pulling apart. By 1960 (Map 9), the center lines were totally separated.

1. The technique for finding the location of each center line was as follows: (a) all of the metropolitan area tracted by 1940 was divided into five roughly equal pie-shaped sectors, the specific boundaries of which were determined by major traffic arteries that, in turn, generally divide groupings of consecutively numbered census tracts; (b) the center of population for each racial group (white and non-white, with 98 percent of the latter being Negro and therefore termed "Negro" for convenience sake) in each sector in the three census years was calculated by standard methods; and (c) for each racial group in each census year, a curve was drawn from sector to sector connecting the sector centers of population. Note: Greater detail in the location of the center lines could be shown by dividing the city into smaller and more numerous sectors, but the general location of the center lines would not be altered by such a procedure.

If Negroes and whites were indeed involved in any significant numbers in a move toward integrated housing, the center lines of the two populations would tend to converge as a reflection of the move. But the center lines cannot reflect that which does not exist. Indeed, the constantly widening gap between the center lines of the white and Negro populations in the Detroit area is a dynamic measure of *increasing* rather than decreasing segregation in housing.

Another measure of increasing segregation is suggested by the data included in Table 1. These data support the following observations:

1. In the City of Detroit—
   a. In 1930, 51 percent of all Negro residents lived in white or predominately white areas.
   b. By 1960, only 15 percent of the Negro residents lived in so-called white areas.
2. In the Detroit Standard Metropolitan Statistical Area—[2]
   a. In 1940, 31 percent of all Negro residents lived in white or predominately white areas.
   b. By 1960, only 15.6 percent of the Negro residents lived in so-called white areas.

Thus, during the thirty years between 1930 and 1960 there was a very sharp decline in the number of Negro Detroiters living in housing areas that may be described as "integrated."

Still another measure of housing segregation trends in the Detroit area is suggested by the data included in Table 2. This table indicates the racial composition of all census tracts from 1940 through 1960. Lines 1 through 8 on the table demonstrate that the mode for Detroit tracts from 1940 through 1960 has been to *remain* predominately Negro (line 1) or predominately white (line 2), or to *become* increasingly, and usually predominately, Negro (lines 3 through 8). The only major exceptions to the rule are those tracts (indicated in line 9) which have a substantial ethnic minority of whites (largely Polish) whose members remain attached to their traditional areas because of their desire to participate in localized ethnic institutions. The only other exceptions are the two tracts (indicated in line 10 of Table 2) which were predominately Negro and are now "Mixed." The explanation is that these two tracts constitute the urban renewal area known as Lafayette Park, thus substantiating the phrase, "Urban renewal means Negro removal."

Considered in toto, then, Table 2 indicates that housing segregation changes in the Detroit area between 1940 and 1960 were in the direction of an *increase*, rather than toward a decrease, of the phenomenon. Out of a

2. 1930 is not considered in this and in some subsequent parts of the analysis because the suburban areas were not tracted until the 1940 census.

TABLE 1

NUMBER AND PERCENT OF NEGROES AND WHITES LIVING IN NEGRO AND WHITE AREAS, DETROIT STANDARD METROPOLITAN STATISTICAL AREA, 1930-1960

Part A

	NUMBER							
	1930		1940		1950		1960	
	White	Negro	White	Negro	White	Negro	White	Negro
DETROIT AND ENCLAVES								
Negro Ghetto*	1,330	19,908	1,843	37,476	4,157	106,013	4,245	113,786
Predominately Negro	17,267	41,473	33,703	66,429	45,017	117,420	113,255	305,494
Predominately White	602,059	62,497	419,499	47,857	456,703	79,479	346,322	75,376
White Ghetto	923,301	1,787	1,113,537	2,011	1,120,084	1,765	778,244	428
Total	1,534,957	125,665	1,568,582	153,773	1,626,861	304,677	1,242,066	495,084
DETROIT AND SUBURBS								
Negro Ghetto	**	**	1,935	41,879	4,621	131,793	4,588	136,426
Predominately Negro	**	**	38,470	70,799	49,570	123,310	118,359	311,214
Predominately White	**	**	431,209	48,563	489,979	80,781	402,456	82,930
White Ghetto	**	**	1,426,321	2,861	1,778,982	3,619	2,032,064	2,057
Total			1,897,935	164,082	2,323,152	339,503	2,557,467	532,627

Part B

PERCENT

	1930 White	1930 Negro	1940 White	1940 Negro	1950 White	1950 Negro	1960 White	1960 Negro
DETROIT AND ENCLAVES								
Negro Ghetto*	—	15.8	—	24.4	—	34.8	—	23.0
Predominately Negro	1.1	33.0	2.1	43.2	2.8	38.5	9.1	61.8
Predominately White	39.0	49.8	26.7	31.1	28.1	26.1	28.0	15.2
White Ghetto	59.9	1.4	71.2	1.3	69.1	.6	62.9	—
Total	100.0	100.0	100.0	100.0	100.0	100.0	100.0	100.0
DETROIT AND SUBURBS								
Negro Ghetto	**	**	.1	25.5	.2	38.8	.2	25.6
Predominately Negro	**	**	2.0	43.2	2.1	36.3	4.6	58.4
Predominately White	**	**	22.7	29.6	21.1	23.8	15.7	15.6
White Ghetto	**	**	75.2	1.7	76.6	1.1	79.5	.4
Total	**	**	100.0	100.0	100.0	100.0	100.0	100.0

*Negro Ghetto: 90 percent and over Negro; Predominately Negro: 50-89.9 percent Negro; Predominately White: 1-49.9 percent Negro; White Ghetto: less than one percent Negro.
**Suburban areas not tracted until 1940.

7

total of 484 census tracts, 438—or 91 percent—have either remained almost totally segregated or have become increasingly dominated by Negroes (a trend which has always ended in total segregation). The suburbs have remained even more rigidly segregated; only one percent of the 88 suburban tracts have undergone any significant racial change (line 6, Table 2).

TABLE 2

RACIAL COMPOSITION OF CENSUS TRACTS, DETROIT STANDARD METROPOLITAN
STATISTICAL AREA, 1940-1960

	CENSUS YEAR			NUMBER OF CENSUS TRACTS		
	1940	1950	1960	Detroit	Suburbs	Total
1.	N*	N	N	31	4	35
2.	W*	W	W	145	78	223
3.	M*	N	N	25	—	25
4.	M	M	N	35	—	35
5.	W	W	N	25	—	25
6.	W	M	M	23	1	24
7.	W	W	M	49	—	49
8.	W	M	N	24	—	24
9.	M	M	M	34	5	39
10.	N	N	M	2	—	2

*CODE: "N" indicates tracts with 50 percent or more Negroes (a racial composition that has always meant, sooner or later, total dominance by Negroes). "W" indicates tracts with less than one percent Negro. "M" indicates tracts with 1-49.9 percent Negroes.

NOTE: All but three of 484 tracts in the metropolitan area are included in this table. The three tracts not included are in the two (No. 1 and 507) constituting the Central Business District; and one apartment house district (tract 758) where the number of Negroes hovers just above and below one percent, a shift which —due to the category sizes used for this report—would spuriously suggest racial change.

READING THIS TABLE: Line 1 of the table shows that there were 31 Detroit and 4 suburban census tracts, for a total of 35 tracts, which had 50 percent or more Negroes (indicated by the symbol "N") in all three of the census years (1940, 1950 and 1960); Line 2 shows that a total of 223 tracts were less than one percent Negro (indicated by the symbol "W") in all three of the census years; Line 3 shows that 25 tracts were 1-49.9 percent Negro in 1940 (indicated by the symbol "M"), and became more than 50 percent Negro in 1950 and 1960; etc.

The magnitude of the entire phenomenon is conveyed by the following apparently paradoxical generalizations:

1. During the twenty year period, the Detroit city Negro population *increased* by 333,000, yet every Negro area *lost* in total population.

2. During the twenty year period, the Detroit city white population *decreased* by 290,000, yet the only sub-areas which increased in population were those termed "all white."

Both generalizations can only be explained by a mass movement of white residents away from areas where Negroes have lived or into which Negroes have migrated. The result has been the creation of two cities bearing a single name: One, Negro, located in the central city and occupying housing built before 1930; the other, white, now located in the suburbs and on the fringes of the central city and occupying the housing built after 1930.[3]

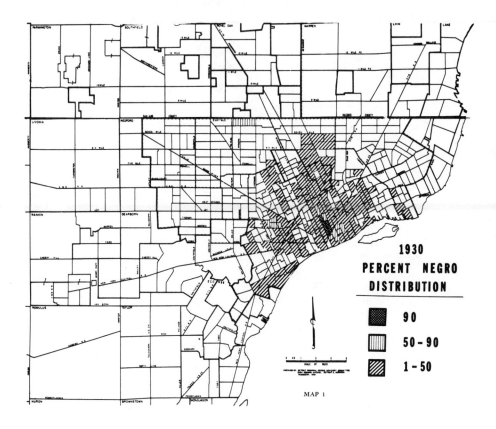

1930
PERCENT NEGRO
DISTRIBUTION

▓ 90
▥ 50 - 90
▨ 1 - 50

MAP 1

3. See Harry Sharp and Leo F. Schnore, "The Changing Color Composition of Metropolitan Areas," Land Economics, 38 (May, 1962), pp. 169-185, for evidence that housing segregation in the Detroit area is representative rather than unique.

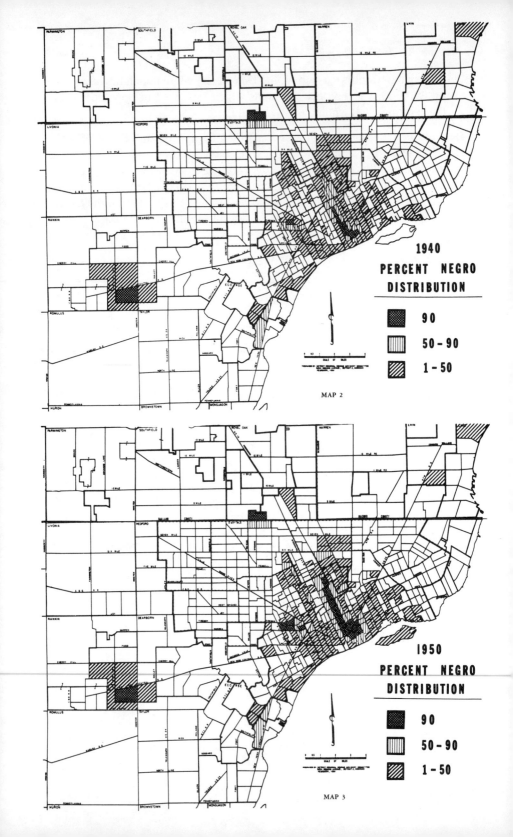

1940
PERCENT NEGRO
DISTRIBUTION

90
50 - 90
1 - 50

MAP 2

1950
PERCENT NEGRO
DISTRIBUTION

90
50 - 90
1 - 50

MAP 3

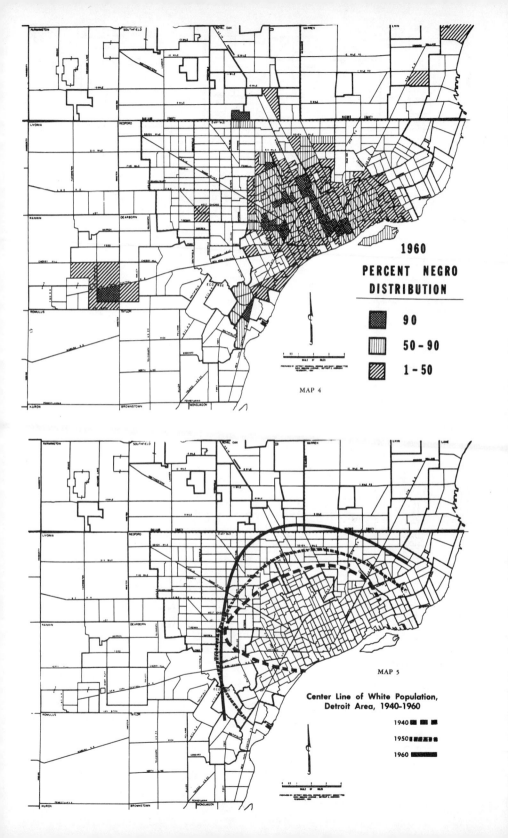

1960

PERCENT NEGRO
DISTRIBUTION

90

50 - 90

1 - 50

MAP 4

MAP 5

Center Line of White Population,
Detroit Area, 1940-1960

1940

1950

1960

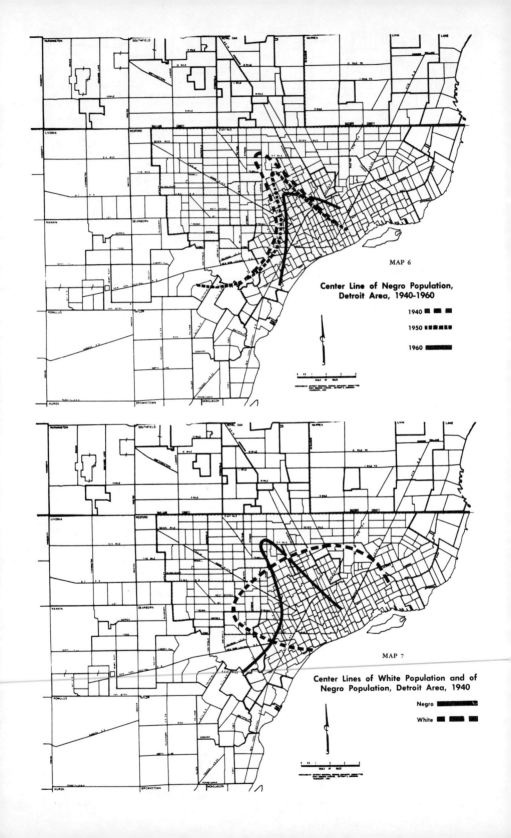

MAP 6

Center Line of Negro Population,
Detroit Area, 1940-1960

1940
1950
1960

MAP 7

Center Lines of White Population and of
Negro Population, Detroit Area, 1940

Negro
White

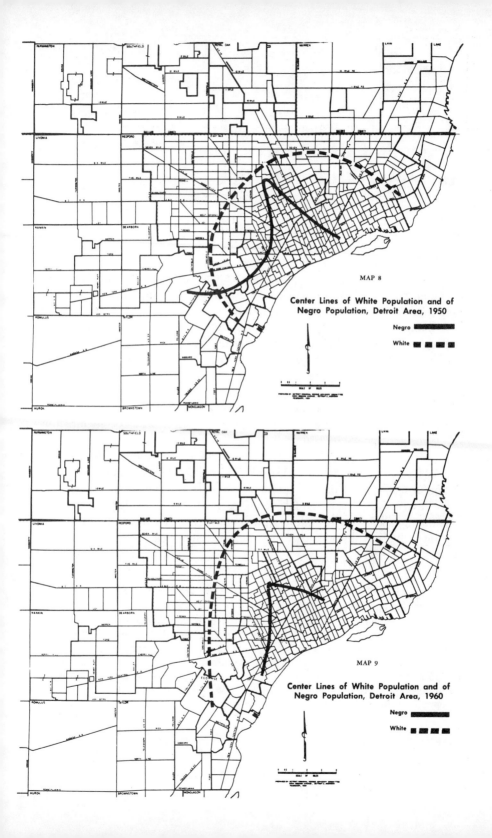

MAP 8

Center Lines of White Population and of
Negro Population, Detroit Area, 1950

Negro ▬▬▬▬
White ▬ ▬ ▬ ▬

MAP 9

Center Lines of White Population and of
Negro Population, Detroit Area, 1960

Negro ▬▬▬▬
White ▬ ▬ ▬ ▬

"Race and Residence" Reviewed After the Riot

Thomas F. Hoult

There are few more aggravating statements than the self-righteous pronouncement titling this article.* "I don't like to say it," says Mr. Smug, "but if you'll remember, I *told* you so long ago."

Smug or not, the importance of the subject prompts me to follow up the suggestion of a colleague. We met at the recent American Sociological Association national convention in San Francisco. His first words to me were, "I've been looking for your article."

"What article?"

"Detroit! You're in a perfect spot to say 'I told you so.' "

The story began more than five years ago when I was associate director of Detroit's Wayne State University Institute of Regional and Urban Studies (IRUS). The director, Albert J. Mayer, and I completed a 1962 study titled "Race and Residence in Detroit," which showed that housing segregation in the city had increased steadily since 1930. This finding prompted my wife to suggest "Pads and Prejudice" as an appropriate title for the study. The finding also strongly undercut the then current assumption that increasing integration is an adequate indicator of improving race relations. We wrote:

Negro Detroiters are more segregated in their housing today than they were three decades ago.

Available data prove this point beyond question, although the statement itself may seem surprising to those who have witnessed the "invasion" of one "white" neighborhood after another. . . . The apparent discrepancy is explained by this simple fact: As Detroit's Negro population has increased, it has spilled out to occupy housing available in adjacent areas. . . . Thus many Caucasian neighborhoods have been "invaded," giving rise to the idea that those who believe in open housing were being fulfilled at last.

*This article by Professor Hoult originally appeared as "About Detroit . . . We Told You So," in *The Crisis* 74, no. 8 (October, 1967), 407-410. Reprinted by permission.

But such invaded neighborhoods do not remain integrated; indeed, in the history of Detroit, the "tipping point" has been as low as five percent. That is, when a so-called white Detroit neighborhood is "invaded" by Negroes, practically all whites flee to outlying areas when the invading group constitutes five percent of the neighborhood population. Entire sub-areas such as Russell Woods (90% Jewish middle class in 1955 and now 90% Negro) undergo almost total racial change in just a few years.

"Race and Residence . . ." was followed by a companion study which it seemed appropriate to title, "The Population Revolution in Detroit." Our reward for this study was to be fired from our IRUS positions. It was nothing short of *revolutionary,* we pointed out, that Detroit was fast becoming a city of dependents—dependents who must be supported on a constantly shrinking tax base. We reported that by 1970, present trends continuing, the city's population would:

> include *only one-quarter* of the most productive age-group (25-44 years) of all persons living in the metropolitan area;
> include *only one-third* of all producing-age persons (15-65 years) living in the metropolitan area;
> have an age distribution such that *between one-third and one-half* (41%) of its total will consist of persons in the age-groups considered generally non-productive (under 15 and over 64 years of age).

To these projections we added the observation that the revolutionary effects of such population change would be accentuated by accompanying alterations in the relative size of the city's two major racial groups. By 1970, we predicted, Detroit would (present trends continuing):

> be approximately 44% Negro in its total population; have a school population that is almost two-thirds Negro (63%);
> have only 18% of all white metropolitan area residents in the child-bearing ages (15-44 years);
> include only one-seventh (15%) of the most productive age-group (25-44 years) of all white persons living in the metropolitan area;
> have 91% of the metropolitan area's aged Negroes (those 65 years of age and over).

These figures were publicized just a week before a major school bond election. The timing was particularly unfortunate for us because, when the bond election lost by 120,000 votes, Dr. Mayer and I were given total "credit." In one sense, we never felt so powerful, but when the press brickbats started flying, we began to feel the mixed benefits of such power. We were accused of political naivete, if not chicanery. It was claimed that the study was released without "proper authorization." And, it was said, publication of the study was done in too flamboyant a manner.

Perhaps there was something to the second charge. Instead of writing the study in jargon and then burying it in some obscure professional journal, we issued it in the form of a sprightly little pamphlet that could be read by intelligent laymen. Also, we hired an artist to design a dramatic cover and he succeeded so well the we were favored with whispers about "commie influence." This charge arose because the artist depicted—in bright red against the white background—a vague gathering of people which, it was said, looked like the stereotype of a cell meeting. Also in red was the word *revolution,* which was printed as if it had been painted roughly on a wall.

The charge about publication without authorization had no substance, but it led to our release nonetheless. We became the scapegoats of a complex power play involving urban renewal land, city officialdom, and research resources at the university. In another situation, it became clear that the city officials were more eager to maintain their reputations than to face reality. Under sub-contract, we had done a study of the attitudes of people with sufficient income to make them potentials for urban renewal housing. When the findings were reported to the city—findings which included the dismaying fact that 95% of affluent white Detroit area residents are not interested in urban renewal housing if it is "open"—the response of the city fathers was, in effect: "If you want to get paid for the report, remove all references to Negroes." They feared the consequences if potential builders learned how limited the market really is when it comes to urban renewal housing.

With "Population Revolution. . . ." harassment took the form of a denial that we had cleared the manuscript with the appropriate university vice president. We had, but he said he "couldn't remember," and the result was that we were released from our IRUS positions and then all support was removed from IRUS itself. The organization has never been reactivated and thus was ended a threat to the prevailing views of a "do-nothing significant" establishment.

The trends revealed in "Population Revolution. . . ." presented the City Fathers with a clear choice: Take some positive steps to alter the effects of the trends or else expect to suffer the consequences in the form of radical civil turmoil. The choice the Fathers made was to strike out at those who forecast trouble.

Meanwhile, the city marched inexorably toward the summer of 1967— the summer which, in effect, we had predicted early in 1963. We concluded "Population Revolution. . . ." with these words:

The purpose of this study has been to describe past events (1940-1960) and to forecast future events (1960-1970) so that those concerned with the city's welfare can take appropriate action. . . .

Present population trends in the Detroit area . . . clearly demonstrate that the city is, by and large, being abandoned by all except those who suffer from relatively great housing, education, and general economic deprivation. . . . By 1970, officials of the City of Detroit will be called upon to give greatly increased social and economic services to a population having greatly decreased opportunities for providing even minimal tax revenues.

These facts, and the almost inevitable conclusion to which they lead . . . suggest that America's great cities, Detroit among them, now must pay for the long-standing American tendency to segregate and to discriminate against minority groups, particularly Negroes.

And now the riot is "over"—along with the loss of 43 lives and something close to fifty million dollars' damage. There are other cities where social scientists have pinpointed the consequences of present trends.* Are the officials of such cities, like those in Detroit, making big-talk about convention centers and International Villages and thus diverting attention from what really needs to be done? If so, then it takes no gift of prophecy to predict racial turmoil in the future.

---

*EDITOR'S NOTE: For national urban documentation of racial segregation residential patterns see: Donald O. Cowgill, "Trends in Residential Segregation in American Cities, 1940-1950," *American Sociological Review* 21 (1956):43-47, and Karl Taeuber, "Negro Residential Segregation: Trends and Measurements," *Social Problems* 12 (1964):42-51.

Attempts to Bridge the Racial Gap
The Religious Establishment

Leonard Gordon

. . . if the church has any real claim to moral leadership, it must speak out clearly and in unity. It must act forcefully and quickly.[1]

This is the conclusion of John Lewis' address to a university audience in May, 1968. Aimed at the role of institutional religion and the race issue generally, it is also a statement of relevance to any consideration of the religious establishment's response to the racial crisis in Detroit, particularly since the riots of July, 1967. The inner-city conditions and interracial tensions that gave rise to this outburst in Detroit are manifestly prevalent throughout urban communities in every region in our society. Consequently, the effectiveness of the religious institutions in Detroit "act(ing) forcefully and quickly" is of general interest.

With respect to the Detroit riot, the initial religious institutional response was quick and coordinated. Twenty-four hours after this most disastrous of racial riots in Detroit and American urban history[2] began on July 23, 1967, an Interfaith Emergency Center (IEC) was formed by representatives of the local Archdiocese, Council of Churches, Jewish Community Council, and All-Black Interdenominational Ministerial Alliance. Around the clock operating headquarters were set up in the Episcopal Dio-

This account draws upon material and experiences of the author accumulated during five years' service, 1962 to 1967, as co-secretary of the Metropolitan Detroit Religion and Race Conference. The professional position held for most of this period was that of Michigan Area Director, American Jewish Committee. This article is previously unpublished.

1. John Lewis, "Religion and Human Rights: A Final Appeal to the Church," *New South* 23, no. 2 (1968):61.
2. The relatively high amount of destruction is graphically made clear in the section entitled "Charts on Levels of Violence and Negotiations" which records the degrees of violence in twenty-four different cities that experienced rioting including Detroit, in the *Report of the National Advisory Commission on Civil Disorders* (New York: Bantam Books, 1968), pp. 583-631.

cese located in midtown Detroit within the general riot area and in close proximity to the heaviest burning, sniping, and police-military activity. Catholic and Protestant churches and the one synagogue in the widespread riot area were activated to serve as distribution points for medical and food needs.

The structural and functional role of what became the ongoing Interfaith Action Council (IAC) can be divided into three phases. These are (1) the pre-riot period during which there occurred the formation and development of the Metropolitan Detroit Religion and Race Conference which provided an organizational structure and ongoing interreligious communications base, (2) the emergence of the Interfaith Emergency Center during the riot crisis, and (3) the development of an ongoing Interfaith Action Council as a direct outgrowth of the IE Center's activities. This latter phase has resulted in an ongoing, functioning, interreligious unit designed to serve in a catalytic role by operating between the inner-city ghetto and establishment leadership. The IAC has a budget and assigned staff from the original sponsors of the Religion and Race Conference.[3] Developments in the initial stage when the Religion and Race Conference was established directly influenced the nature of the religious leadership response during and after the riot when the IEC (IAC) operations were set up. It is the purpose of this article to chronicle these developments in regard to the Religion and Race Conference during the period 1962 to the year of the major racial rioting, 1967.

The process leading to the formation of the Metropolitan Detroit Religion and Race Conference began in the early 1960s with antecedents extending back to abortive efforts following the 1943 race riots.[4] Aside from the external pressures of the civil rights movement, there were multiple internal religious social forces involved in moving the separate Catholic, Jewish, and Protestant establishments to act together. These included the traditional activities of the Jewish community relations network, always operating on the principle of working with social allies whenever possible, and the emergent Protestant concern with a growing black constituency in Detroit that was highly discontented. However, the most dynamic development was the emergence of Vatican II and the Ecumenical Movement under the influence of Pope John XXIII, whose picture is featured in the outer foyer of Detroit Archbishop Deardon's* offices in downtown Detroit. One

---

*Now Cardinal.
3. The Rev. Arlie E. Porter and Father James J. Sheehan, "Proposal for an Interfaith Action Council," mimeographed, October 1967.
4. Alfred McClung Lee and Norman Raymond Humphrey, "The Interracial Committee of the City of Detroit: A Case History," *The Journal of Educational Sociology* 19, no. 5 (1946), 278-288.

local consequence was the emergence in 1962 of the Detroit Archbishop's
Committee on Human Relations whose Director, Father James Sheehan,
initiated communications with representatives of the local Council of
Churches and Jewish Community Council.[5]

This internal religious community development corresponded with a
rising tide of civil rights activity and growing inner-city discontent. Symptomatic was the NAACP leadership then under the professional direction of
Arthur Johnson* and lay leadership of Edward Turner. These men were
helping to develop a more direct action approach to civil rights beyond judicial and educational efforts. Demonstrations for better education, housing,
employment, and general equality of treatment and opportunity began,
leading up to the 100,000 June, 1963, Detroit march led by Martin Luther
King. As Mr. Johnson reflected at a Religion and Race Conference meeting
during this period, he felt as Dr. King did the now classic refrain that he and
his organization had to run to keep up with his people because he was their
leader. At this time growing numbers of people were looking to other organizations such as CORE and the Saul Alinsky-advised West Central Organization. The former attracted the kind of middle-class Negroes that in the
past looked to the NAACP and the latter gathered a following of the lower
socioeconomic Negroes who traditionally have been organizationally unin-
volved in civil rights activities.

Challenges to Early Operational Assumptions

Once interreligious communications links were established during the
early 1960s in Detroit, the most immediate point of discussion was the
problems associated with race. The initial focus was on raising moral issues
and then mounting educational campaigns for the various religious constituencies and the public generally. The initial assumptions made were based
upon the conviction, to be later sharply challenged by events, that racial
divisiveness in the community could largely be overcome by reminding
people of their respective religious teachings. Within this assumption was
the feeling that the vast majority of the three religious constituencies deeply
felt the moral dilemma on race that Gunnar Myrdal postulated in the 1940s
in his encyclopedic *An American Dilemma*.[6] The idea that the masses of

---

*Mr. Johnson is presently Deputy Superintendent of the Detroit Public School System.
5. The organizational genesis of what became the Detroit Religion and Race Conference is discussed by Abraham Citron, ed., in the introduction of *Challenge to Conscience* (Detroit: The Detroit Metropolitan Conference on Religion and Race, 1963),
pp. 1-3.
6. Gunnar Myrdal, *An American Dilemma: The Negro Problem and Modern Democracy* (New York: Harper and Brothers Publishers, 1944).

white Catholics, Jews, and Protestants were basically conscious-stricken at the dual feelings of commitment to universal human dignity embedded in the Judaeo-Christian ethic while living in a racially divided and prejudicial community was accepted at face value. The passage of a "closed occupancy" proposal by a 54% to 46% general vote margin in 1964, after a major effort by the religious leadership joined by the United Auto Workers, Democratic Party leadership, and others organized in an *ad hoc* "Citizens for a United Detroit" organization, was one of a series of developments that served to demonstrate to religious leaders that for most whites no serious moral dilemma existed.[7] A majority of whites simply opposed equality of opportunity for Negroes, even after an intensive educational effort was made in the churches and synagogues and in the community generally to oppose a specific segregationist ordinance. The conclusion of the Report of the National Advisory Commission on Civil Disorders (Kerner Commission) on white racism in Detroit and other riot-stricken communities was a recognizable fact several years prior to the riots of 1967.[8]

Another mistaken assumption was that the religious establishment could operate unilaterally on racial justice without a working relationship with Negroes. This became evident in the process of developing the Religion and Race Conference's first programmatic step. This was the formation of an Open Occupancy Conference in the fall of 1962.[9] This Conference was structured as a tri-sponsored organization by the metropolitan Detroit Archdiocese, Council of Churches, and Jewish Community Council. Each group was to have four representatives, and the first chairman was the late Reverend Donald Schroeder of the Council of Churches. The focus of concern in the early stages of the Conference did not include a participative planning or programmatic role with black leadership. This was to be challenged so sharply and importantly that lessons were available to learn about new assertive black leadership. The ongoing plans for the Conference illustrate this.

The initial plans for an Open Occupancy Conference were laid during the gubernatorial campaign of 1962. A two-day conference was scheduled for January 2 and 3, 1963, at the University of Michigan Rackham Memorial in Detroit to which the religious leadership invited the newly elected

---

7. James J. Sheehan, "Human Dignity," *The Archbishop's Committee on Human Relation's Newsletter* (Detroit) 2, no. 1 (1964): 2.
8. Discussing the basic causes of the Detroit and other racial riots in 1967 and earlier the Commission on Civil Disorders concluded that "white racism is essentially responsible for the explosive mixture which has been accumulating in our cities since the end of World War II." See: *Report of the National Advisory Commission on Civil Disorders,* op. cit., p. 203.
9. Citron, op. cit., pp. 1-3.

governor for a keynote address. This invitation was extended prior to the November elections and both the then Democratic Governor John Swainson and the Republican governor-to-be George Romney agreed to appear. By December the conference plans were finalized with the assistance of the Detroit Commission on Community Relations which, ironically, was initially formed as a response to the 1943 Detroit riots.[10] The program was to include, along with George Romney's first address as Governor of Michigan and a series of discussion workshops, speeches on moral commitment by theological representatives of the three religious co-sponsors.[11]

The issue of black participation was raised parenthetically at an early fall Open Occupancy Conference meeting by Executive Committee member Dr. Abe Citron, the early formulator of the Conference theme. It was the consensus of the Executive Committee that since it was whites who were keeping blacks from the open housing market, it was the job of whites to teach other whites their moral duty. After this there was no further consideration of black participation until December when representatives of various black leadership organizations, including the Interdenominational Ministerial Alliance and the NAACP, informed the Conference Executive Committee that a black boycott of the Conference was planned, including picketing at the Conference. The Conference by this time was gaining considerable news coverage, but this rather dynamic development never reached the mass media or the general public. A 6:00 A.M. private "summit" breakfast meeting was quickly set up in mid December at the Wolverine Hotel in downtown Detroit. The Conference Executive Committee was informed by more than a dozen prominent Negro leaders that they would not support any program, whatever its aims or sponsors, that affected the human dignity and social rights of blacks unless they were equal participants in the planning process and on the program. The Conference Executive Committee accepted this view with dispatch. The immediate response was to bring specific black community leaders into the conference. The Reverend Charles W. Butler of the Interdenominational Ministerial Alliance was placed on the program as a featured speaker. Willie Baxter, a labor negotiator and later a member of Mayor Jerome Cavanagh's administration, was made a member of the Executive Committee. Arthur Johnson, the then Michigan Executive Secretary of the NAACP, was placed on the Committee on Conclusions and Recommendations. The Open Occupancy Conference was held as scheduled on January 2-3, 1963.

10. Lee and Humphrey, op. cit., pp. 278-288.
11. Citron, op. cit., pp. 8-18.

Emergence of the Continuing Religion and Race Conference

Less than a month after the Detroit-based conference, the first National Religion and Race Conference was held in Chicago. In response the Detroit Open Occupancy Conference shifted its name to Religion and Race, adding the Greek Orthodox Diocese as a constituent member.[12] The internal organizational structure was now comprehensively representative of the religious establishment in Detroit. The Protestants included among their lay representatives Lawrence Washington, Negro and a successful executive of one of the automotive firms. The Reverend Joseph Pelham, first suburban Negro minister, was to be added in 1964 as was Horace Sheffield of the United Auto Workers Union hierarchy. To use contemporary terminology, not then generally employed, these were Establishment Black leadership. It was not then clearly perceived by members of the Religion and Race Executive Committee what the Kerner Commission highlighted, that is, that establishment black leadership never had a large following in the Negro community.[13] Not recognized was the depth of social disorganization and feelings of alienation and free-floating hostility, accentuated by the civil rights movement.

That this perception was based on reality is made evident by the findings of two Wayne State University sociologists who reported (see part one) that the line of residential separation between the races had been increasing for over three decades.[14] This growing gap was paralleled in other demographically measured black and white differences, as income and educational levels. It is evident that while the middle-class black community was closing the gap, the mass of blacks in the lower socioeconomic levels were falling relatively farther behind.[15]

The program of the Religion and Race Conference between 1962 and 1967 was aimed generally at reducing interracial tensions by a "challenge to conscience."[16] This challenge was largely thrust at the white middle class of the metropolitan area and was, in effect, an effort to assist middle-class blacks to move into the larger community. The inner-city ghetto areas per se were not a programmatic focus. Thus, the first conference's aim

---

12. Shmarya Kleinman, "The Religion and Race Conference," Minutes of the Community Relations Committee of the Jewish Community Council of Metropolitan Detroit, meeting of September 25, 1963, p. 3.
13. *Report . . . ,* op. cit., pp. 235-236.
14. Albert Mayer and Thomas Hoult, *Race and Residence in Detroit* (Detroit: Wayne State University Institute for Urban Studies, 1962).
15. Hanna H. Meissner, *Poverty in the Affluent Society* (New York: Harper and Row Publishers, 1966), p. 51.
16. This was the theme of the first Religion and Race Conference, see Citron, op. cit.

in 1963 of open occupancy if fully implemented would have been applicable to that small part of the Negro community that could afford outer-city and suburban housing. This represented less than one-quarter of the half million black community in Detroit.[17] A follow-up suburban conference in 1964 in the wealthy suburb of Birmingham had a similar aim.[18] In the year 1964 this approach continued with a major political effort to defeat a Detroit Homeowners Ordinance which was designed to maintain racially segregated neighborhoods in Detroit.[19]

The manifest aims of the Religion and Race Conference were not achieved in any significant manner during these years, Detroit's positive reputation in these years of the early and mid sixties notwithstanding.[20] The events in the summer of 1967 poignantly made this clear. Blacks in the inner-city ghetto situation were growing more, not less, alienated.[21] However, there were latent consequences to the functioning of the Conference that were to be activated during the riots. This development was related to the close informal as well as formal communication links established by the various religious organizational staff and lay representatives to the Conference over a five-year period of regularly meeting. The rapport developed in this process was directly related to the rapidity with which the Interfaith Emergency Center was operationally set up in July of 1967.

A Static Period

By early 1967 the Religion and Race Conference was operating on little else than a communications level with monthly meetings at the downtown

17. John Musial, *Midwestern Minority Housing Markets* (Detroit: Advance Mortgage Corporation, 1962).

18. *Archbishop's Committee on Human Relation's Newsletter* (Detroit) 1, no. 6 (1964):2-3.

19. Sheehan, op. cit. The view many white Detroiters had about the meaning of residential integration is evident from a radio exchange of views between the author, representing the Citizens for a United Detroit (CUD), and Thomas Poindexter, representing the Greater Detroit Homeowners Council (GDHC). In the tape of this program, provided by the United Auto Workers, it was noted that one provision of the "homeowners ordinance" proposed by the GDHC would have given a homeowner the right to maintain "congenial surroundings for himself, his family and tenants." How the representative of the GDHC viewed new black residents in the neighborhood surroundings is evident by his statement in the program that "it is essential to the future of Detroit that this flight to the suburbs be halted by reassuring the homeowners of neighborhood stability against the spread of crime, disease and neighborhood blight." As noted in the text, the ordinance passed, but it was declared unconstitutional in the courts. This conflict in Detroit was mirrored in 1964 in California where voters adopted a constitutional amendment which voided a fair housing law enacted by the state legislature.

20. As Mayor Jerome Cavanagh stated in mid May 1967, two months prior to the July disorders, "enlightened policies have spared Detroit the civil upheavals that have struck other cities," see: Lukas, J. Anthony, "Postscript on Detroit: Whitey Hasn't Got the Message," *The New York Times Magazine,* August 27, 1967, p. 48.

21. Ibid., pp. 24-25 and 41-58.

Detroit Jewish Welfare Federation Butzel Building. The only newsworthy activity was a name change from "Religion and Race" to "Religion and Human Rights," proposed by Presbyterian Minister Robert Hoppe, an Executive Committee Member.[22]

The one planned project, discussed between mid 1965 and mid 1967, was to develop plans for a Crime Conference. Mayor Cavanagh's opponent for reelection in 1965, Walter Shamie, touched a major white community anxiety by stressing the "crime in the streets" issue.[23] The Conference plan was to focus the white community's attention on the underlying problems of cultural deprivation and alienation that gave rise to much of criminal behavior, particularly as it was manifested in the inner-city black community. Hard enforcement issues such as "stop and frisk" laws and unequal enforcement procedures were to be considered. Besides religious leadership, the program was to include participation from academic, business, labor, and government communities.[24]

It was this last participant category that proved the major stumbling block. Continuous unsuccessful attempts to finalize the program pointed up a disquieting aspect of Mayor Jerome Cavanagh's administration by the mid sixties. The mayor was no longer available for direct meetings or consultation as he was in 1961 when first elected. He simply could not be reached. The early dramatic years of the Cavanagh administration had seen the development of a series of glittering successes, including the Model Cities concept and a new dimension of rapport with the black community. By the mid sixties Mayor Cavanagh had become a national figure and his position as president of the Mayor's Conference carried him and his attention out of Detroit.[25] Then his unsuccessful attempt to defeat former governor G. Mennen Williams in the 1966 senatorial primary split the Democratic Party in Detroit, particularly after Williams was defeated by Republican Robert Griffin for the Senate.[26] Although the mayor's office is officially nonpartisan, this pragmatically alienated a major portion of the mayor's support. One result was a void in effective leadership at City Hall.

---

22. From the file notes of the author. For a clear statement of Rev. Hoppe's views see: Robert A. Hoppe, "An Interview with ——," in the *Archbishop's Committee on Human Relation's Newsletter* (Detroit) 2, no. 5 (1965):1.

23. Without citing Mr. Shamie directly this issue was written about by Burton Levy, Director of Community Services for the Michigan Civil Rights Commission, in the *Archbishop's Committee on Human Relation's Newsletter* 3, no. 1 (1965): 4-5; see also Lukas, op. cit., p. 58.

24. One of the Consultants in plans for this proposed conference was George Edwards, former Detroit Police Chief, whose views were considered particularly constructive. These views were stated by Mr. Edwards in his *The Police on the Urban Frontiere* (New York: Institute on Human Relations, 1968).

25. Lukas, op. cit., p. 48.

26. Ibid., p. 58.

The Religion and Race Conference's lack of initiative with or without communication of the mayor's office was symptomatic of a malaise of underlying discontent that was setting into Detroit by the mid sixties. There was the well-documented growing residential distance between blacks and whites. The Model Cities concept initially was designed primarily to assist the inner-city disadvantaged. Instead, when too limited resources were allotted, priority developments resulted in urban renewal programs that displaced thousands of poor blacks, as new expressways, new governmental structures, new business enterprises, and new expensive high-rise apartments went up. This resulted in increasing density and discontent in the inner city.[27]

Detroit was plunging toward the violence of July, 1967. The one substantive accomplishment of religious leadership in Detroit was to establish the kind of communication links not evident in reports of other riot-torn cities.[28]

Development of New Operating Assumptions

The July, 1967, riot had the immediate effect of sharply shifting the religious leadership's perspective on the racial issue. With the emergence of the Interfaith Emergency Council to meet immediate food and medical needs there was a transition away from concentration upon moral education which was a characteristic of the Religion and Race Conference. The new posture was that of direct social action as provided during the riots and that of serving as a catalyst to direct social action by the constituencies of the Catholic, Jewish, and Protestant religious groupings. This catalytic posture was made explicit several weeks after the riots in a statement to the Executive Committee of the Interfaith Emergency (later Action) Council by one of its working committees:

1. We, of the Interfaith Emergency Council, serve two constituencies: The inner-city community and the outer-city/suburban community. The first is predominantly Negro, the second predominantly white. The two constituencies have different current needs, different points of view.
2. The Roman Catholic, main-line Protestant, and Jewish groups are white, with only a small percentage of exceptions.
3. The white constituency, being generally middle class and relatively privileged, does not understand the meaning of the riot because it does not yet understand

27. As noted in *Race and Residence in Detroit* "urban renewal (often) means Negro removal" resulting in increased concentration of predominantly black residential areas, see: Mayer and Hoult, op. cit., p. 13.
28. See: *Report of the National Advisory Commission on Civil Disorders,* op. cit. For a detailed account of one typical city—Los Angeles—in which interracial communication links were for all practical purposes nonexistent see: Robert Conot, *Rivers of Blood, Years of Darkness* (New York: Bantam Books, 1967).

Negro needs, aims, and frustrations any more than it understands the plight of the poor in American society.

4. We, the metropolitan area religious leaders, must seek to speak to both constituencies—inner-city and outer-city/suburban—but our first responsibility is to interpret the riot to our white constituencies, as it throws light on the whole constellation of urban problems. To the inner-city community we must strive to make demonstrably clear that religious groups actively support them in their efforts to be free men and to enjoy all the rights of life and citizenship in an affluent society. Our role here is supportive.

The Negro must be recognized and treated as a man . . . a free man . . . and participate fully in all aspects of the decision making processes in American life. This right must be especially recognized in working on three major problems which are as yet unsolved: (1) An adequate supply of good housing for all income levels and along with this, an open housing market throughout the metropolitan area. (2) Many more jobs at all levels of management and at all degrees of skill or professionalism, plus retraining hard core jobless persons. (3) Quality education for all children of the Detroit area, which means in realistic terms, substantially more revenue to enable the schools to do as good a job as educators can be trained to provide.

[As an immediate step] we recommend that Suburban Action Centers be established in the North, Northwest, West and Southwest sections of our metropolitan area. These centers, with full-time staff and supporting clerical personnel, would provide a stimulus for a massive expansion of church and community human relations information, educational, and attitudinal change programming."[29]

This statement to the Interfaith Emergency Council represented a radical shift on the race issue for religious leadership in Detroit on two grounds. One was the wider range of specific proposals in the areas of housing, jobs, and education. The second was a new, clear concern with the underclass of the black community, for example, "the hard-core unemployed." The issue of open occupancy was not dropped, but like the crime conference proposal, there was implicit recognition that the old perspective was from middle-class whites to middle-class blacks (indeed at the beginning of the Religion and Race Conference the communication was from middle-class whites to middle-class whites). The religious leadership in Detroit had begun for the first time to look at the core issues in black-white relations. Whites in the suburbs who are a specific focus in the above IEC statement represent the community's economic, political, and social power structure even as the political dimension to this power is being challenged.[30] Blacks in the inner city represent the mass of the discontented city residents.

29. Joseph L. Hansknecht, "Statement on the Detroit Riot, with Recommended Actions for Churches and Synagogues," Constituency Committee, Interfaith Emergency Council, mimeographed, 1967, pp. 1-2.
30. Donald Lief, "Elections," *City: Bi-Monthly Review of Urban America* 2, no. 1 (1968):8-11.

The effectiveness of the organized religious community in implementing its new perspective by serving as a social catalyst between inner-city blacks and outer-city middle-class whites can only be determined over a period of time. And time is a commodity of which there may be little if interracial accommodation in Detroit, and elsewhere, is to become a reality.

Messages About a Racially
Divided Community

EDITOR'S NOTE: The first three of the next four articles are based upon addresses of Mayor Jerome P. Cavanagh, Richard Marks, and the Reverend Charles Butler at the 1963 Open Occupancy Conference sponsored by The Detroit Metropolitan Conference on Religion and Race. The full report of the conference is available in *Challenge to Conscience*, Report of the Metropolitan Detroit Conference on Open Occupancy.

Message to the Open Occupancy Conference

*Mayor Jerome P. Cavanagh**

It is most significant and gratifying that the first major religious conference of this new year meets to confront a basic problem of urban life.

Your belief in open occupancy is demonstrated by your assembling here. The impact of your statements, your decisions, and your specific action plans can meaningfully bolster the image of metropolitan Detroit. It is only through the cooperative effort of leadership representing every segment of this great urban complex that we will make the dream of Detroit—equality, used in its broadest sense—a living reality.

The Federal Housing Act of 1949 sets forth as the national objective of a comprehensive housing program, "the realization of a decent home in a good living environment for every American family as soon as possible." The scope of federal programs has widened during this past decade, and under President Kennedy's recent Executive Order, no American can be denied the right to enjoy these benefits because of race, creed, color, or national origin.

Our goals on the local level can be no less than this. As we plan and rebuild a new Detroit through participation in the federally-supported urban

*Mr. Cavanagh was mayor of Detroit at the time these remarks were made January 2, 1963.

29

renewal program, we have the opportunity to change the face of our city, to remove blight with all of its negative components.

Policies which do nothing to equalize opportunities in housing will have grave consequences for economic, governmental, political, religious, and educational institutions. By persuasion and other means, we must work to remove artificial barriers which place members of certain racial, ethnic, or religious groups at a disadvantage.

OPEN OCCUPANCY represents a challenge to conscience and a challenge to government.

Detroit has its slums and blight, its areas of great density, and like every major industrial city of the North, its pattern of racially-segregated housing. Whether through deliberate design, ignorance, or apathy, the movement of some of our citizens has been restricted on a racial, religious, and at times nationality basis. There exists a pattern of discrimination. Those who have contributed to the growth and vitality of this community continue to suffer from the effects of these inequities. The growing minority population desires, and has been seeking, additional and improved housing within our community.

An important and necessary outcome of this conference is that civic and religious leadership rededicate itself to the creation of a moral and social climate encompassing the full acceptance of all people. Equality of treatment must be the keystone of our community's spirit.

We are building a better Detroit, and conferences such as this can expedite the process of breaking with those traditions which limit and restrict. We can equally choose to motivate and encourage participation in, and full enjoyment of, our society. This must be an inclusive America for all citizens.

Message to the Open Occupancy Conference

*Richard V. Marks**

We live in a metropolitan area composed of four million people— roughly one-half of these people live in the City of Detroit; the other half live in the tri-county area outside the city. As of 1960, in *that* so-called suburban area, a total nonwhite population of 80,000 is to be found living and located in the same census tracts that they were in 1940. These patterns were maintained despite the tremendous new housing construction that has taken place in the metropolitan region. Except for some recent developments

*Mr. Marks was Executive Director of the Detroit Commission on Community Relations at the time these remarks were made.

in the Pontiac area, the pattern can only be described as segregated and restrictive.

With reference to Detroit's nonwhite population, it has grown from 150,000 in 1940 to 303,000 in 1950 to 487,000 in 1960. This is a total population that is over twice the size of Michigan's second largest city, Grand Rapids.

In 1940, some seven basic clusters of nonwhite population could be identified in separate and distinct residential areas in the City of Detroit. Many other areas reflected the presence of nonwhites. In 1950, the number of separate and distinct community areas where 1,000 or more nonwhites lived had increased to eleven. Each of the previous clusters had increased in size of area covered and in the number of people included. By 1960, a more evident concentration of nonwhite residents was apparent, and a general shift toward the near northwest section of Detroit was becoming increasingly evident. But for the most part these areas of nonwhite residence were the same as those recognized in 1940, with the difference that they now have merged into two huge basic clusters. The process of neighborhood succession is revealed in the shifting composition of population *within* areas that have long been identified as having nonwhite occupancy.

The percentage of Negroes in Detroit rose from less than 10% in 1940 to almost 30% in 1960, while the percentage in the suburbs decreased from 5% to 3%. This occurred at a time when suburban areas were experiencing the greatest mass housing construction and population shifts in our century. In view of the massive population increases and even more massive population movements in Detroit and the metropolitan area, one can reasonably conclude that there is no such thing as population and housing stability. Relative to race, the distribution of nonwhite population reflects unequal housing opportunities. The sobering reality of this period of population movement in Detroit was not integration, but succession. In the words of one student of the subject ". . . integration is usually a term to describe the period of time that elapses between the appearance of the first Negro and the exit of the last white."

This brings us up to 1960. We find Detroit is made up of almost 555,000 housing units, 130,000 of which are occupied by nonwhites. If the trends that we have experienced during the last ten years continue into the future, each year some 6,500 homes currently occupied by whites will be transferred to nonwhite ownership. If housing opportunities continue to be restricted, these transfers will occur almost entirely in the City of Detroit. In the coming ten-year period this will mean some 65,000 dwelling units will change from white to nonwhite occupancy. Add to this several thousand additional dwelling units that will be transferred as a result of displacement from urban renewal sites, expressway construction, and new schools and parks. The bulk of these activities will affect nonwhite citizens and add to the total demand for additional homes during this next ten-year period. It should be mentioned that direct access to *new* housing would substantially reduce the necessity for white to nonwhite housing transfers, thus promoting racial stabilization and dispersion.*

Only one question remains—where will these housing opportunities be found? Will the past be but prologue to the future? What will be the resultant patterns that emerge from the interplay of the three factors: a rising middle-class nonwhite home-seeker, the not-so-impersonal housing industry and market, and those of us who control the available housing supply and the spirit of welcome?

The threatening tragedy of our present situation is that the patterns of the past can all too easily be repeated and extended, thus producing a grossly segregated city within an even more segregated metropolitan area. Such a consequence will only further aggravate the existing racial divisions, misunderstandings, and hostilities that plague us today.

To our eternal credit we have learned from our errors of the past. There is an ever-growing consensus among the different groups in our society that open occupancy, the right of equal housing opportunities, is the only thing to do—that it is right not only for individuals but for institutions which have equally identified the moral and economic issues involved. Open occupancy, then, is not a goal which we can *tolerate* as being more desirable than a system of discrimination; it is a goal that we are coming to recognize as one that we must *deliberately seek* for our individual, our neighborhood, and our institutional survival.

Message to the Open Occupancy Conference

Rev. Charles W. Butler†

The pamphlet "Race and Residence in Detroit" published six months ago by the Urban Research Laboratory, Institute for Urban Studies, Wayne State University, opens with these words: "Negro Detroiters are more segregated in their housing today than they were three decades ago."

The external problem can be summarized as the fourfold housing alliance of builder, broker, owner, and banker to keep the ethnic belt at the

---

*EDITOR'S NOTE: At the time of this writing—mid 1970—preliminary U.S. Census data returns indicate a trend toward the beginnings of a black movement into the suburbs in Detroit and elsewhere. This movement seems to be in clusters of concentration in older suburbs which points to a continued segregation pattern but more dispersed than in the past.

†Mr. Butler represented Detroit's black Interdenominational Ministerial Alliance when making these remarks.

"normal" position. This alliance is not unlike the former alliance of breeder, buyer, boss in the economy of slavery. It is in reality an extension and refinement of the latter with the same basic goal, control, especially control of mobility, and the control of the mind. E. Franklin Frazier, in *The Black Bourgeoisie,* lists immobility as one of the marks of slavery. Indeed, he who is denied freedom of movement by one is, to that extent, slave to that one.

Mobility must mean both the right and the ability to move freely. The desire and the right to move without the ability to move is cruel and frustrating. . . . On the other hand, the desire and ability to move without the right to move is refined slavery. . . .

The contradiction here apparent between democratic practices and democratic theories has far-reaching, if not corrosive, influences on the effectiveness of our international affairs.

The internal problems rising from the ghetto are concomitant to the external problems and cannot be fully reflected in tables of statistics. The immobility occasioned thereby does grievous, if not abiding, damage to the personalities of those trapped in this web. It is a silent, yet very real, method of achieving the same psychological conditioning that resulted when the slave compared his shanty with the "big house" of the master. . . . The product is essentially the same, the propagation of a sense of inferiority. . . . Here is spawned and cultivated the spirit of rebellion against that in which one is, but to which one feels little or no sense of belonging. This rebellion is evident in many forms, from nonviolent resistance to vandalism. This rebellion is proof positive that the Negro has grown weary of being the eternal afterthought of America. . . .

Message to the Grass Roots

EDITOR'S NOTE: In late 1963, the Detroit Council for Human Rights announced a Northern Negro Leadership Conference to be held in Detroit on November 9 and 10. As noted in the introduction, when the council's chairman, Rev. C. L. Franklin, sought to exclude black nationalists and Freedom Now Party advocates from the conference, Rev. Albert B. Cleage, Jr., resigned from the council and, in collaboration with the Group On Advanced Leadership (GOAL), arranged for a Northern Negro Grass Roots Leadership Conference. This convened in Detroit at the same time as the more conservative gathering, which was addressed by Congressman Adam Clayton Powell among others. The two-day rally was held at the King Solomon Baptist Church, with Rev. Cleage, journalist William Worthy, and Malcolm X as the chief speakers. The audience, almost all black and with non-Muslims in the great majority, interrupted Malcolm X with applause and laughter so often that he asked it to desist because of the lateness of the hour.

A few weeks after the conference President Kennedy was assassinated and Elijah Muhammad silenced Malcolm X as a Black Muslim spokesman. This is, therefore, one of the last speeches Malcolm X gave before leaving Muhammad's organization. It is not a typical Black Muslim speech. Even though Malcolm X continued to preface certain statements with the phrase, "The Honorable Elijah Muhammad says," he was increasingly, in the period before the split, giving his own special stamp to the Black Muslims' ideas. Included at this stage of his career was the idea of separation.

The following selection, printed by permission, consists of about one-half of the speech. The long-playing record, "Message to the Grass Roots by Malcolm X" published by the Afro-American Broadcasting and Recording Company, Detroit, is vastly superior to the written text in conveying the style and personality of Malcolm X at his best—when he was speaking to a militant black audience.

Malcolm X

We want to have just an off-the-cuff chat between you and me, us. We want to talk right down to earth in a language that everybody here can easily understand. We all agree tonight, all of the speakers have agreed, that America has a very serious problem. Not only does America have a very serious problem, but our people have a very serious problem. America's problem is us. We're her problem. The only reason she has a problem is she doesn't want us here. And every time you look at yourself, be you black, brown, red or yellow, a so-called Negro, you represent a person who poses such a serious problem for America because you're not wanted. Once you face this as a fact, then you can start plotting a course that will make you appear intelligent, instead of unintelligent.

What you and I need to do is learn to forget our differences. When we come together, we don't come together as Baptists or Methodists. You don't catch hell because you're a Baptist, and you don't catch hell because you're a Methodist. You don't catch hell because you're a Methodist or a Baptist, you don't catch hell because you're an American, because if you were an American, you wouldn't catch hell. You catch hell, all of us catch hell, for the same reason.

So we're all black people, so-called Negroes, second-class citizens, ex-slaves. You're nothing but an ex-slave. You don't like to be told that. But what else are you? You are ex-slaves. You didn't come here on the "Mayflower." You came here on a slave ship. In chains, like a horse, or a cow, or a chicken. And you were brought here by the people who came here on the "Mayflower," you were brought here by the so-called Pilgrims, or Founding Fathers. They were the ones who brought you here.

We have a common enemy. We have this in common: We have a common oppressor, a common exploiter, and a common discriminator. But once we all realize that we have a common enemy, then we unite—on the basis of what we have in common. And what we have foremost in common is that enemy—the white man. He's an enemy to all of us. I know some of you think that some of them aren't enemies. Time will tell.

In Bandung back in, I think, 1954, was the first unity meeting in centuries of black people. And once you study what happened at the Bandung conference, and the results of the Bandung conference, it actually serves as a model for the same procedure you and I can use to get our problems solved. At Bandung all the nations came together, the dark nations from Africa and Asia. Some of them were Buddhists, some of them were Muslims, some of them were Christians, some of them were Confucianists, some were atheists. Despite their religious differences, they came together. Some were communists, some were socialists, some were capitalists—despite their economic and political differences, they came together. All of them were black, brown, red, or yellow.

The number-one thing that was not allowed to attend the Bandung conference was the white man. He couldn't come. Once they excluded the white man, they found that they could get together. Once they kept him out, everybody else fell right in and fell in line. This is the thing that you and I have to understand. And these people who came together didn't have nuclear weapons, they didn't have all of the heavy armaments that the white man has. But they had unity.

They were able to submerge their little petty differences and agree on one thing; That there one African came from Kenya and was being colonized by the Englishman, and another African came from the Congo and was being colonized by the Belgian, and another African came from Guinea and was being colonized by the French, and another came from Angola and was being colonized by the Portuguese. When they came to the Bandung conference, they looked at the Portuguese, and at the Frenchman, and at the Englishman, and at the Dutchman, and learned or realized the one thing that all of them had in common—they were all from Europe, they were all Europeans, blond, blue-eyed and white skins. They began to recognize who their enemy was. The same man that was colonizing our people in Kenya was colonizing our people in the Congo. The same one in the Congo was colonizing our people in South Africa, and in Southern Rhodesia, and in Burma, and in India, and Afghanistan, and in Pakistan. They realized all over the world where the dark man was being oppressed, he was being oppressed by the white man; where the dark man was being exploited, he was being exploited by the white man. So they got together on this basis—that they had a common enemy.

And when you and I here in Detroit and in Michigan and in America who have been awakened today look around us, we too realize here in America we all have a common enemy, whether he's in Georgia or Michigan, whether he's in California or New York. He's the same man—blue eyes and blond hair and pale skin—the same man. So what we have to do is what they did. They agreed to stop quarreling among themselves. Any little spat that they had, they'd settle it among themselves, go into a huddle—don't let the enemy know that you've got a disagreement.

Instead of airing our differences in public, we have to realize we're all the same family. And when you have a family squabble, you don't get out on the sidewalk. If you do, everybody calls you uncouth, unrefined, un-civilized, savage. If you don't make it at home, you settle it at home; you get in the closet, argue it out behind closed doors, and then when you come out on the street, you pose a common front, a united front. And this is what we need to do in the community, and in the city, and in the state. We need to stop airing our differences in front of the white man, put the white man out of our meetings, and then sit down and talk shop with each other. That's what we've got to do.

I would like to make a few comments concerning the difference between the black revolution and the Negro revolution. Are they both the same? And if they're not, what is the difference? What is the difference between a black revolution and a Negro revolution? First, what is a revolution? Sometimes I'm inclined to believe that many of our people are using this word "revolution" loosely, without taking careful consideration of what this word actually means, and what its historic characteristics are. When you study the historic nature of revolutions, the motive of a revolution, the objective of a revolution, the result of a revolution, and the methods used in a revolution, you may change words. You may devise another program, you may change your goal and you may change your mind.

Look at the American Revolution in 1776. That revolution was for what? For land. Why did they want land? Independence. How was it carried out? Bloodshed. Number one, it was based on land, the basis of indepen-dence. And the only way they could get it was bloodshed. The French Rev-olution—what was it based on? The landless against the landlord. What was it for? Land. How did they get it? Bloodshed. Was no love lost, was no compromise, was no negotiation. I'm telling you—you don't know what a revolution is. Because when you find out what it is, you'll get back in the alley, you'll get out of the way.

The Russian Revolution—what was it based on? Land; the landless against the landlord. How did they bring it about? Bloodshed. You haven't got a revolution that doesn't involve bloodshed. And you're afraid to bleed. I said, you're afraid to bleed.

As long as the white man sent you to Korea, you bled. He sent you to Germany, you bled. He sent you to the South Pacific to fight the Japanese, you bled. You bleed for white people, but when it comes to seeing your own churches being bombed and little black girls murdered, you haven't got any blood. You bleed when the white man says bleed; you bite when the white man says bite; and you bark when the white man says bark. I hate to say this about us, but it's true. How are you going to be nonviolent in Mississippi, as violent as you were in Korea? How can you justify being nonviolent in Mississippi and Alabama, when your churches are being bombed, and your little girls are being murdered, and at the same time you are going to get violent with Hitler, and Tojo, and somebody else you don't even know?

If violence is wrong in America, violence is wrong abroad. If it is wrong to be violent defending black women and black children and black babies and black men, then it is wrong for America to draft us and make us violent abroad in defense of her. And if it is right for America to draft us, and teach us how to be violent in defense of her, then it is right for you and me to do whatever is necessary to defend our own people right here in this country.

The Chinese Revolution—they wanted land. They threw the British out, along with the Uncle Tom Chinese. Yes, they did. They set a good example. When I was in prison, I read an article—don't be shocked when I say that I was in prison. You're still in prison. That's what America means: prison. When I was in prison, I read an article in *Life* magazine showing a little Chinese girl, nine years old; her father was on his hands and knees and she was pulling the trigger because he was an Uncle Tom Chinaman. When they had the revolution over there, they took a whole generation of Uncle Toms and just wiped them out. And within ten years that little girl became a full-grown woman. No more Toms in China. And today it's one of the toughest, roughest, most feared countries on this earth—by the white man. Because there are no Uncle Toms over there.

Of all our studies, history is best qualified to reward our research. And when you see that you've got problems, all you have to do is examine the historic method used all over the world by others who have problems similar to yours. Once you see how they got theirs straight, then you know how you can get yours straight. There's been a revolution, a black revolution, going on in Africa. In Kenya, the Mau Mau were revolutionary; they were the ones who brought the word "Uhuru" to the fore. The Mau Mau, they were revolutionary, they believed in scorched earth, they knocked everything aside that got in their way, and their revolution also was based on land, a desire for land. In Algeria, the northern part of Africa, a revolution took place. The Algerians were revolutionists, they wanted land. France offered to let them be integrated into France. They told France, to hell with France, they wanted some land, not some France. And they engaged in a bloody battle.

So I cite these various revolutions, brothers and sisters, to show you that you don't have a turn-the-other-cheek revolution. There's no such thing as a nonviolent revolution. The only kind of revolution that is nonviolent is the Negro revolution. The only revolution in which the goal is loving your enemy is the Negro revolution. It's the only revolution in which the goal is a desegregated lunch counter, a desegregated theater, a desegregated park, and a desegregated public toilet; you can sit down next to white folks—on the toilet. That's no revolution. Revolution is based on land. Land is the basis of all independence. Land is the basis of freedom, justice, and equality.

The white man knows what a revolution is. He knows that the black revolution is world-wide in scope and in nature. The black revolution is sweeping Asia, is sweeping Africa, is rearing its head in Latin America. The Cuban Revolution—that's a revolution. They overturned the system. Revolution is in Asia, revolution is in Africa, and the white man is screaming because he sees revolution in Latin America. How do you think he'll react to you when you learn what a real revolution is? You don't know what a revolution is. If you did, you wouldn't use that word.

Revolution is bloody, revolution is hostile, revolution knows no compromise, revolution overturns and destroys everything that gets in its way. And you, sitting around here like a knot on the wall, saying, "I'm going to love these folks no matter how much they hate me." No, you need a revolution. Whoever heard of a revolution where they lock arms, as Rev. Cleage was pointing out beautifully, singing "We Shall Overcome"? You don't do that in a revolution. You don't do any singing, you're too busy swinging. It's based on land. A revolutionary wants land so he can set up his own nation, an independent nation. These Negroes aren't asking for any nation—they're trying to crawl back on the plantation.

When you want a nation, that's called nationalism. When the white man became involved in a revolution in this country against England, what was it for? He wanted this land so he could set up another white nation. That's white nationalism. The American Revolution was white nationalism. The French Revolution was white nationalism. The Russian Revolution too —yes, it was—white nationalism. You don't think so? Why do you think Khrushchev and Mao can't get their heads together? White nationalism. All the revolutions that are going on in Asia and Africa today are based on what? —black nationalism. A revolutionary is a black nationalist. He wants a nation. I was reading some beautiful words by Rev. Cleage, pointing out why he couldn't get together with someone else in the city because all of them were afraid of being identified with black nationalism. If you're afraid of black nationalism, you're afraid of revolution. And if you love revolution, you love black nationalism.

To understand this, you have to go back to what the young brother here referred to as the house Negro and the field Negro back during slavery. There were two kinds of slaves, the house Negro and the field Negro. The house Negroes—they lived in the house with master, they dressed pretty good, they ate good because they ate his food—what he left. They lived in the attic or the basement, but still they lived near the master; and they loved the master more than the master loved himself. They would give their life to save the master's house—quicker than the master would. If the master said, "We got a good house here," the house Negro would say, "Yeah, we got a good house here." Whenever the master said "we," he said "we." That's how you can tell a house Negro.

If the master's house caught on fire, the house Negro would fight harder to put the blaze out than the master would. If the master got sick, the house Negro would say, "What's the matter, boss, *we* sick?" *WE* sick! He identified himself with his master, more than his master identified with himself. And if you came to the house Negro and said, "Let's run way, let's escape, let's separate," the house Negro would look at you and say, "Man, you crazy. What you mean, separate? Where is there a better house than this? Where can I wear better clothes than this? Where can I eat better food than this?" That was that house Negro. In those days he was called a "house nigger." And that's what we call them today, because we've still got some house niggers running around here.

This modern house Negro loves his master. He wants to live near him. He'll pay three times as much as the house is worth just to live near his master, and then brag about "I'm the only Negro out here." "I'm the only one on the job." "I'm the only one in this school." You're nothing but a house Negro. And if someone comes to you right now and says, "Let's separate," you say the same thing that the house Negro said on the plantation. "What you mean, separate? From America, this good white man? Where you going to get a better job than you get here?" I mean, this is what you say. "I ain't left nothing in Africa," that's what you say. Why, you left your mind in Africa.

On that same plantation, there was the field Negro. The field Negroes—those were the masses. There were always more Negroes in the field than there were Negroes in the house. The Negro in the field caught hell. He ate leftovers. In the house they ate high up on the hog. The Negro in the field didn't get anything but what was left of the insides of the hog. They call it "chitt'lings" nowadays. In those days they called them what they were—guts. That's what you were—gut-eaters. And some of you are still gut-eaters.

The field Negro was beaten from morning to night; he lived in a shack, in a hut; he wore old, castoff clothes. He hated his master. I say he hated his master. He was intelligent. That house Negro loved his master, but that field Negro—remember, they were in the majority, and they hated the master. When the house caught on fire, he didn't try to put it out; that field Negro prayed for a wind, for a breeze. When the master got sick, the field

Negro prayed that he'd die. If someone came to the field Negro and said, "Let's separate, let's run," he didn't say "Where we going?" He'd say, "Any-place is better than here." You've got field Negroes in America today. I'm a field Negro. The masses are the field Negroes. When they see this man's house on fire, you don't hear the little Negroes talking about "*our* govern-ment is in trouble." They say, "*The* government is in trouble." Imagine a Negro: "*Our* government"! I even heard one say "*our* astronauts." They won't even let him near the plant—and "*our* astronauts"! "*Our* Navy"—that's a Negro that is out of his mind, a Negro that is out of his mind.

Just as the slavemaster of that day used Tom, the house Negro, to keep the field Negroes in check, the same old slavemaster today has Negroes who are nothing but modern Uncle Toms, twentieth-century Uncle Toms, to keep you and me in check, to keep us under control, keep us passive and peaceful and nonviolent. That's Tom making you nonviolent. It's like when you go to the dentist, and the man's going to take your tooth. You're going to fight him when he starts pulling. So he squirts some stuff in your jaw called Novocaine, to make you think they're not doing anything to you. So you sit there and because you've got all of that Novocaine in your jaw, you suffer—peacefully. Blood running all down your jaw, and you don't know what's happening. Because someone has taught you to suffer—peacefully.

The white man does the same thing to you in the street, when he wants to put knots on your head and take advantage of you and not have to be afraid of your fighting back. To keep you from fighting back, he gets these old religious Uncle Toms to teach you and me, just like Novocaine, to suffer peacefully. Don't stop suffering—just suffer peacefully. As Rev. Cleage pointed out, they say you should let your blood flow in the streets. This is a shame. You know he's a Christian preacher. If it's a shame to him, you know what it is to me.

There is nothing in our book, the Koran, that teaches us to suffer peace-fully. Our religion teaches us to be intelligent. Be peaceful, be courteous, obey the law, respect everyone; but if someone puts his hand on you, send him to the cemetery. That's a good religion. In fact, that's that old-time religion. That's the one that Ma and Pa used to talk about: an eye for an eye, and a tooth for a tooth, and a head for a head, and a life for a life. That's a good religion. And nobody resents that kind of religion being taught but a wolf, who intends to make you his meal.

This is the way it is with the white man in America. He's a wolf—and you're sheep. Any time a shepherd, a pastor, teaches you and me not to run from the white man and, at the same time, teaches us not to fight the white man, he's a traitor to you and me. Don't lay down a life all by itself. No, preserve your life, it's the best thing you've got. And if you've got to give it up, let it be even-Stephen.

The slavemaster took Tom and dressed him well, fed him well and even gave him a little education—a *little* education; gave him a long coat and a top hat and made all the other slaves look up to him. Then he used Tom to control them. The same strategy that was used in those days is used today, by the same white man. He takes a Negro, a so-called Negro, and makes him prominent, builds him up, publicizes him, makes him a celebrity. And then he becomes a spokesman for Negroes—and a Negro leader.

I would like to mention just one other thing quickly, and that is the method that the white man uses, how the white man uses the "big guns," or Negro leaders, against the Negro revolution. They are not a part of the Negro revolution. They are used against the Negro revolution.

When Martin Luther King failed to desegregate Albany, Georgia, the civil-rights struggle in America reached its low point. King became bankrupt almost, as a leader. The Southern Christian Leadership Conference was in financial trouble; and it was in trouble, period, with the people when they failed to desegregate Albany, Georgia. Other Negro civil-rights leaders of so-called national stature became fallen idols. As they became fallen idols, began to lose their prestige and influence, local Negro leaders began to stir up the masses. In Cambridge, Maryland, Gloria Richardson; in Danville, Virginia, and other parts of the country, local leaders began to stir up our people at the grass-roots level. This was never done by these Negroes of national stature. They control you, but they have never incited you or excited you. They control you, they contain you, they have kept you on the plantation.

As soon as King failed in Birmingham, Negroes took to the streets. King went out to California to a big rally and raised I don't know how many thousands of dollars. He came to Detroit and had a march and raised some more thousands of dollars. And recall, right after that Roy Wilkins attacked King. He accused King and CORE (Congress Of Racial Equality) of starting trouble everywhere and then making the NAACP (National Association for the Advancement of Colored People) get them out of jail and spend a lot of money; they accused King and CORE of raising all the money and not paying it back. This happened; I've got it in documented evidence in the newspaper. Roy started attacking King, and King started attacking Roy and (James) Farmer started attacking both of them. And as these Negroes of national stature began to attack each other, they began to lose their control of the Negro masses.

The Negroes were out there in the streets. They were talking about how they were going to march on Washington. Right at that time Birmingham had exploded, and the Negroes in Birmingham—remember, they also exploded. They began to stab the crackers in the back and bust them up 'side their head—yes, they did. That's when Kennedy sent in the troops, down in Birmingham. After that, Kennedy got on the television and said "this is a moral issue." That's when he said he was going to put out a civil-rights bill. And when he mentioned civil-rights bill and the Southern crackers started talking about how they were going to boycott or filibuster it, then the Negroes started talking—about what? That they were going to march on Washington, march on the Senate, march on the White House, march on the Congress, and tie it up, bring it to a halt, not let the government proceed. They even said they were going out to the airport and lay down on the runway and not let any airplanes land. I'm telling you what they said. That was revolution. That was revolution. That was the black revolution.

It was the grass roots out there in the street. It scared the white man to death, scared the white power structure in Washington, D.C., to death; I was there. When they found out that this black steamroller was going to come down on the capital, they called in Wilkins, they called in (A. Philip) Randolph, they called in these national Negro leaders that you respect and told them, "Call it off." Kennedy said, "Look, you all are letting this thing go too far." And Old Tom said, "Boss, I can't stop it, because I didn't start it." I'm telling you what they said. They said, "I'm not even in it, much less at the head of it." They said, "These Negroes are doing things on their own. They're running ahead of us." And that old shrewd fox, he said, "If you all aren't in it, I'll put you in it. I'll put you at the head of it. I'll endorse it. I'll welcome it. I'll help it. I'll join it."

A matter of hours went by. They had a meeting at the Carlyle Hotel in New York City. The Carlyle Hotel is owned by the Kennedy family; that's the hotel Kennedy spent the night at, two nights ago; it belongs to his family. A philanthropic society headed by a white man named Stephen Currier called all the top civil-rights leaders together at the Carlyle Hotel. And he told them, "By you all fighting each other, you are destroying the civil-rights movement. And since you're fighting over money from white liberals, let us set up what is known as the Council for United Civil Rights Leadership. Let's form this council, and all the civil-rights organizations will belong to it, and we'll use it for fund-raising purposes." Let me show you how tricky the white man is. As soon as they got it formed, they elected Whitney Young as its chairman, and who do you think became the co-chairman? Stephen Currier, the white man, a millionaire. (Adam Clayton) Powell was talking about it down at Cobo Hall today. This is what he was talking about. Powell knows it happened. Randolph knows it happened. Wilkins knows it happened. King knows it happened. Every one of that Big Six—they know it happened.

Once they formed it, with the white man over it, he promised them and gave them $800,000 to split up among the Big Six; and told them that after the march was over they'd give them $700,000 more. A million and a half dollars—split up between leaders that you have been following, going to jail for, crying crocodile tears for. And they're nothing but Frank James and Jesse James and the what-do-you-call-'em brothers.

As soon as they got the setup organized, the white man made available to them top public-relations experts; opened the news media across the country at their disposal, which then began to project these Big Six as the leaders of the march. Originally they weren't even in the march. You were talking this march talk on Hastings Street, you were talking march talk on Lenox Avenue, and on Fillmore Street, and on Central Avenue, and 32nd Street and 63rd Street. That's where the march talk was being talked. But the white man put the Big Six at the head of it; made them the march. They became the march. They took it over. And the first move they made after they took it over, they invited Walter Reuther, a white man; they invited a priest, a rabbi, and an old white preacher, yes, an old white preacher. The same white element that put Kennedy into power—labor, the Catholics, the Jews, and liberal Protestants; the same clique that put Kennedy in power, joined the march on Washington.

It's just like when you've got some coffee that's too black, which means it's too strong. What do you do? You integrate it with cream, you make it weak. But if you pour too much cream in it, you won't even know you ever had coffee. It used to be hot, it becomes cool. It used to be strong, it becomes weak. It used to wake you up, now it puts you to sleep. This is what they did with the march on Washington. They joined it. They didn't integrate it, they infiltrated it. They joined it, became a part of it, took it over. And as they took it over, it lost its militancy. It ceased to be angry, it ceased to be hot, it ceased to be uncompromising. Why, it even ceased to be a march. It became a picnic, a circus. Nothing but a circus, with clowns and all. You had one right here in Detroit—I saw it on television—with clowns leading it, white clowns and black clowns. I know you don't like what I'm saying, but I'm going to tell you anyway. Because I can prove what I'm saying. If you think I'm telling you wrong, you bring me Martin Luther King and A. Philip Randolph and James Farmer and those other three, and see if they'll deny it over a microphone.

No, it was a sellout. It was a take-over. When James Baldwin came in from Paris, they wouldn't let him talk, because they couldn't make him go by the script. Burt Lancaster read the speech that Baldwin was supposed to make; they wouldn't let Baldwin get up there, because they know Baldwin is liable to say anything. They controlled it so tight, they told those Negroes what time to hit town, how to come, where to stop, what signs to carry, what song to sing, what speech they could make, and what speech they couldn't make; and then told them to get out of town by sundown. And every one of those Toms was out of town by sundown. Now I know you don't like my saying this. But I can back it up. It was a circus, a performance that beat anything Hollywood could ever do, the performance of the year. Reuther and those other three devils should get an Academy Award for the best actors because they acted like they really loved Negroes and fooled a whole lot of Negroes. And the six Negro leaders should get an award too, for the best supporting cast.

The Riot Period

editor's commentary

The three articles in part two provide a graphic description of the 1967 riot that stemmed from the growing interracial tensions in Detroit.

The first selection from the Kerner Commission report is a detailed account of the events of July 23 to July 27, 1967.[1] Following this is a researched interpretation by Robert Mendelsohn of why the conflict happened. Mendelsohn began collecting his data shortly after the riot and conducted extensive interviews with both blacks and whites. His findings revealed that low status and rural background, generally presumed to be crucial factors in such disorders, were not major explanatory variables. Instead he found that the arrestees' unemployment records and other social characteristics were "roughly equal to the black community as a whole." In addition, Mendelsohn found that the rioters "like most Negro Detroiters . . . are not recent arrivals." There was found to be a correlation between age, particularly the early twenties, and participation in the riot. His central finding is that when the riot participants and sympathizers are considered together, it is clear that the black community as a whole is deeply dissatisfied with their social position, as opposed to "status," in the general community. Mendelsohn makes this clear when he observes that "in summary, the conditions of life for the Negro-American are not acceptable anywhere in the United States, regardless of whether the city is considered a disaster like Newark or a 'model city' as Detroit was once characterized." This finding parallels that of Warren's in part three based upon more extensive random sampling data collected a year after the riot.

The third article in part two, by Thomas Forrest, continues the consideration of the religious institutional responses to the riot, the background of which is presented in Gordon's article in part one. The genesis and operational activity of the Interfaith Emergency Center (IEC) is of interest because it represented the only operational and somewhat effective communal response during the riot crisis. As Forrest documents, the regular private and governmental social welfare agencies were not functioning along with the rest of the private and governmental sectors of the community. The IEC became the catalytic social agent and coordinator of efforts of the United Auto Workers union and some private businesses to bring needed emergency goods and services to people in the riot-disrupted parts of the city. The Forrest article is based upon his work at the Ohio State University Disaster Research Center which apparently views racial riots as

---

1. For a well-documented book-length account of the riot see: Hubert Locke, *The Detroit Race Riot of 1967* (Detroit : Wayne State University Press, 1969.)

natural disasters, the centers' original research concern. It represents an empirical accounting of organizational emergence and institutionalization in a community conflict context.

The riot contained a number of cues about the specific nature of race relations in Detroit. This observer was in the riot area most of the time during the riot, working out of the IEC. It was evident that neither was the sniping activity nor the looting a random process. Attacks were directed at symbols of coercive and economic authority in the white community. As in Watts where over 100 police cars and fire-fighting equipment were damaged or destroyed,[2] the sniping attacks were directed not at whites generally, for example, those returning from a Tiger baseball game, but at policemen and firemen and their equipment. In the first two days of the riot, looting and fire bombing of stores was selective. Those with "soul brother" signs were often bypassed, and some chain stores were selected while others with a better reputation for fair treatment were neglected. This pattern was not clearly discernible by the third day of the riot as whole blocks of businesses went up in flames and/or were looted. A further point of social import is that, as Mendelsohn's article denotes and other analyses independently confirm,[3] sniping and looting participants in the riot came more or less equally from all income brackets. The riot demonstrated in this process the alienation of large portions of the entire black community. Low socioeconomic status as an independent variable, then, is joined by race as an independent variable in the aggressive discontent within the black community.

2. Russell Dynes and Enrico Quarantelli, "What Looting in Civil Disturbances Really Means," in James F. Short, Jr., ed., *Modern Criminals* (New York: Aldine Publishing Company, 1970), p. 189.
3. Ibid., pp. 189-190.

Profile of the Disorder

On Saturday evening, July 22, the Detroit Police Department raided five "blind pigs." The blind pigs had had their origin in prohibition days, and survived as private social clubs. Often, they were after-hours drinking and gambling spots.

The fifth blind pig on the raid list, the United Community and Civic League at the corner of 12th Street and Clairmount, had been raided twice before. Once 10 persons had been picked up; another time, 28. A Detroit Vice Squad officer had tried but failed to get in shortly after 10 o'clock Saturday night. He succeeded, on his second attempt, at 3:45 Sunday morning.

The Tactical Mobile Unit, the Police Department's Crowd Control Squad, had been dismissed at 3:00 A.M. Since Sunday morning traditionally is the least troublesome time for police in Detroit—and all over the country —only 193 officers were patrolling the streets. Of these, 44 were in the 10th Precinct where the blind pig was located.

Police expected to find two dozen patrons in the blind pig. That night, however, it was the scene of a party for several servicemen, two of whom were back from Vietnam. Instead of two dozen patrons, police found 82. Some voiced resentment at the police intrusion.

An hour went by before all 82 could be transported from the scene. The weather was humid and warm—the temperature that day was to rise to 86—and despite the late hour, many people were still on the street. In short order, a crowd of about 200 gathered.

In November of 1965, George Edwards, Judge of the United States Court of Appeals for the Sixth Circuit, and Commissioner of the Detroit

FROM: "Profiles of Disorder: Detroit," in *Report of the National Advisory Commission on Civil Disorders* (New York: Bantam Books, 1968), pp. 84-108. For a fuller account see: Hubert Locke, *The Detroit Riot of 1967* (Detroit: Wayne State University Press, 1969.)

Police Department from 1961 to 1963, had written in the *Michigan Law Review:*

It is clear that in 1965 no one will make excuses for any city's inability to foresee the possibility of racial trouble. . . . Although local police forces generally regard themselves as public servants with the responsibility of maintaining law and order, they tend to minimize this attitude when they are patrolling areas that are heavily populated with Negro citizens. There, they tend to view each person on the streets as a potential criminal or enemy, and all too often that attitude is reciprocated. Indeed, hostility between the Negro communities in our large cities and the police departments is the major problem in law enforcement in this decade. It has been a major cause of all recent race riots.

At the time of Detroit's 1943 race riot, Judge Edwards told Commission investigators, there was "open warfare between the Detroit Negroes and the Detroit Police Department." As late as 1961, he had thought that "Detroit was the leading candidate in the United States for a race riot."

There was a long history of conflict between the police department and citizens. During the labor battles of the 1930s, union members had come to view the Detroit Police Department as a strike-breaking force. The 1943 riot, in which 34 persons died, was the bloodiest in the United States in a span of two decades.

Judge Edwards and his successor, Commissioner Ray Girardin, attempted to restructure the image of the department. A Citizens Complaint Bureau was set up to facilitate the filing of complaints by citizens against officers. In practice, however, this Bureau appeared to work little better than less enlightened and more cumbersome procedures in other cities.

On 12th Street, with its high incidence of vice and crime, the issue of police brutality was a recurrent theme. A month earlier the killing of a prostitute had been determined by police investigators to be the work of a pimp. According to rumors in the community the crime had been committed by a Vice Squad officer.

At about the same time, the killing of Danny Thomas, a 27-year-old Negro Army veteran, by a gang of white youths, had inflamed the community. The city's major newspapers played down the story in hope that the murder would not become a cause for increased tensions. The intent backfired. A banner story in the *Michigan Chronicle*, the city's Negro newspaper, began:

As James Meredith marched again Sunday to prove a Negro could walk in Mississippi without fear, a young woman who saw her husband killed by a white gang, shouting: "Niggers keep out of Rouge Park," lost her baby.
Relatives were upset that the full story of the murder was not being told, apparently in an effort to prevent the incident from sparking a riot.

Some Negroes believed that the daily newspapers' treatment of the story was further evidence of the double standard: playing up crimes by Negroes, playing down crimes committed against Negroes.

Although police arrested one suspect for murder, Negroes questioned why the entire gang was not held. What, they asked, would have been the result if a white man had been killed by a gang of Negroes? What if Negroes had made the kind of advances toward a white woman that the white men were rumored to have made toward Mrs. Thomas?

The Thomas family lived only four or five blocks from the raided blind pig. A few minutes after 5:00 A.M., just after the last of those arrested had been hauled away, an empty bottle smashed into the rear window of a police car. A litter basket was thrown through the window of a store. Rumors circulated of excess force used by the police during the raid. A youth, whom police nicknamed "Mr. Greensleeves" because of the color of his shirt, was shouting: "We're going to have a riot!" and exhorting the crowd to vandalism.

At 5:20 A.M. Commissioner Girardin was notified. He immediately called Mayor Jerome Cavanagh. Seventeen officers from other areas were ordered into the 10th Precinct. By 6:00 A.M. police strength had grown to 369 men. Of these, however, only 43 were committed to the immediate riot area. By that time the number of persons on 12th Sreet was growing into the thousands and widespread window-smashing and looting had begun.

On either side of 12th Street were neat, middle-class districts. Along 12th Street itself, however, crowded apartment houses created a density of more than 21,000 persons per square mile, almost double the city average.

The movement of people when the slums of "Black Bottom" had been cleared for urban renewal had changed 12th Street from an integrated community into an almost totally black one, in which only a number of merchants remained white. Only 18 percent of the residents were homeowners. Twenty-five percent of the housing was considered so substandard as to require clearance. Another 19 percent had major deficiencies.

The crime rate was almost double that of the city as a whole. A Detroit police officer told Commission investigators that prostitution was so widespread that officers made arrests only when soliciting became blatant. The proportion of broken families was more than twice that in the rest of the city.

By 7:50 A.M., when a 17-man police commando unit attempted to make the first sweep, an estimated 3,000 persons were on 12th Street. They offered no resistance. As the sweep moved down the street, they gave way to one side, and then flowed back behind it.

A shoe store manager said he waited vainly for police for two hours as the store was being looted. At 8:25 A.M. someone in the crowd yelled "The cops are coming!" The first flames of the riot billowed from the store. Firemen who responded were not harassed. The flames were extinguished.

By mid-morning, 1,122 men—approximately a fourth of the police department—had reported for duty. Of these, 540 were in or near the six-block riot area. One hundred and eight officers were attempting to establish a cordon. There was, however, no interference with looters, and police were refraining from the use of force.

Commissioner Girardin said: "If we had started shooting in there . . . not one of our policemen would have come out alive. I am convinced it would have turned into a race riot in the conventional sense."

According to witnesses, police at some roadblocks made little effort to stop people from going in and out of the area. Bantering took place between police officers and the populace, some still in pajamas. To some observers, there seemed at this point to be an atmosphere of apathy. On the one hand, the police failed to interfere with the looting. On the other, a number of older, more stable residents, who had seen the street deteriorate from a prosperous commercial thoroughfare to one ridden by vice, remained aloof.

Because officials feared that the 12th Street disturbance might be a diversion, many officers were sent to guard key installations in other sections of the city. Belle Isle, the recreation area in the Detroit River that had been the scene of the 1943 riot, was sealed off.

In an effort to avoid attracting people to the scene, some broadcasters cooperated by not reporting the riot, and an effort was made to downplay the extent of the disorder. The facade of "business as usual" necessitated the detailing of numerous police officers to protect the 50,000 spectators that were expected at that afternoon's New York Yankee-Detroit Tigers baseball game.

Early in the morning a task force of community workers went into the area to dispel rumors and act as counter-rioters. Such a task force had been singularly successful at the time of the incident in the Kercheval district (near Belle Isle) in the summer of 1966, when scores of people had gathered at the site of an arrest. Kercheval, however, has a more stable population, fewer stores, less population density, and the city's most effective police-community relations program.

The 12th Street area, on the other hand, had been determined, in a 1966 survey conducted by Ernest Harburg of the Psychology Department of the University of Michigan, to be a community of high stress and tension. An overwhelming majority of the residents indicated dissatisfaction with their environment.

Of those interviewed, 93 percent said they wanted to move out of the neighborhood; 73 percent felt that the streets were not safe; 91 percent believed that a person was likely to be robbed or beaten at night; 58 percent knew of a fight within the last 12 months in which a weapon had been employed; 32 percent stated that they themselves owned a weapon; 57 percent were worried about fires.

A significant proportion believed municipal services to be inferior; 36 percent were dissatisfied with the schools; 43 percent with the city's contribution to the neighborhood; 77 percent with the recreational facilities; 78 percent believed police did not respond promptly when they were summoned for help.

United States Representative John Conyers, Jr., a Negro, was notified about the disturbance at his home, a few blocks from 12th Street, at 8:30 A.M. Together with other community leaders, including Hubert G. Locke, a Negro and assistant to the commissioner of police, he began to drive around the area. In the side streets he asked people to stay in their homes. On 12th Street, he asked them to disperse. It was, by his own account, a futile task.

Numerous eyewitnesses interviewed by Commission investigators tell of the carefree mood with which people ran in and out of stores, looting and laughing, and joking with the police officers. Stores with "Soul Brothers" signs appeared no more immune than others.* Looters paid no attention to residents who shouted at them and called their actions senseless. An epidemic of excitement had swept over the persons on the street.

Congressman Conyers noticed a woman with a baby in her arms; she was raging, cursing "whitey" for no apparent reason.

Shortly before noon Congressman Conyers climbed atop a car in the middle of 12th Street to address the people. As he began to speak he was confronted by a man in his fifties whom he had once, as a lawyer, represented in court. The man had been active in civil rights. He believed himself to have been persecuted as a result, and it was Conyers' opinion that he may have been wrongfully jailed. Extremely bitter, the man was inciting the crowd and challenging Conyers: "Why are you defending the cops and the establishment? You're just as bad as they are!"

A police officer in the riot area told Commission investigators that neither he nor his fellow officers were instructed as to what they were supposed to be doing. Witnesses tell of officers standing behind sawhorses as an area was being looted—and still standing there much later, when the mob had moved elsewhere. A squad from the commando unit, wearing hel-

---

*EDITOR'S NOTE: This observer saw a pattern on some blocks in the riot area of looting and fire destruction that was selective until the second day of the four days of intensive rioting.

mets with face-covering visors and carrying bayonet-tipped carbines, block-
aded a street several blocks from the scene of the riot. Their appearance
drew residents into the street. Some began to harangue them and to question
why they were in an area where there was no trouble. Representative Conyers convinced the police department to remove the commandos.

By that time a rumor was threading through the crowd that a man had
been bayoneted by the police. Influenced by such stories, the crowd became
belligerent. At approximately 1:00 P.M. stonings accelerated. Numerous
officers reported injuries from rocks, bottles, and other objects thrown at
them. Smoke billowed upward from four fires, the first since the one at the
shoe store early in the morning. When firemen answered the alarms, they
became the target for rocks and bottles.

At 2:00 P.M. Mayor Cavanagh met with community and political
leaders at police headquarters. Until then there had been hope that, as the
people blew off steam, the riot would dissipate. Now the opinion was nearly
unanimous that additional forces would be needed.

A request was made for state police aid. By 3:00 P.M. 360 officers
were assembling at the armory. At that moment looting was spreading from
the 12th Street area to other main thoroughfares.

There was no lack of the disaffected to help spread it. Although not yet
as hard-pressed as Newark, Detroit was, like Newark, losing population.
Its prosperous middle-class whites were moving to the suburbs and being
replaced by unskilled Negro migrants. Between 1960 and 1967 the Negro
population rose from just under 30 percent to an estimated 40 percent of
the total.

In a decade the school system had gained 50,000 to 60,000 children.
Fifty-one percent of the elementary school classes were overcrowded. Simply
to achieve the statewide average, the system needed 1,650 more teachers
and 1,000 additional classrooms. The combined cost would be $63 million.

Of 300,000 school children, 171,000, or 57 percent, were Negro. According to the Detroit Superintendent of Schools, Dr. Norman Drachler, 25
different school districts surrounding the city spent up to $500 more per
pupil per year than Detroit. In the inner-city schools, more than half the
pupils who entered high school became dropouts.

The strong union structure had created excellent conditions for most
working men, but had left others, such as civil service and government workers, comparatively disadvantaged and dissatisfied. In June the "Blue Flu"
had struck the city as police officers, forbidden to strike, had staged a sick-
out. In September, the teachers were to go on strike. The starting wages for
a plumber's helper were almost equal to the salary of a police officer or
teacher.

Some unions, traditionally closed to Negroes, zealously guarded training opportunities. In January of 1967 the school system notified six apprenticeship trades it would not open any new apprenticeship classes unless a large number of Negroes were included. By fall, some of the programs were still closed.

High school diplomas from inner city schools were regarded by personnel directors as less than valid. In July, unemployment was at a five-year peak. In the 12th Street area it was estimated to be between 12 and 15 percent for Negro men and 30 percent or higher for those under 25.

The more education a Negro had, the greater the disparity between his income and that of whites with the same level of education. The income of whites and Negroes with a seventh-grade education was about equal. The median income of whites with a high school diploma was $1,600 more per year than that of Negroes. White college graduates made $2,600 more. In fact, so far as income was concerned, it made very little difference to a Negro man whether he had attended school for 8 years or for 12. In the fall of 1967, a study conducted at one inner-city high school, Northwestern, showed that, although 50 percent of the dropouts had found work, 90 percent of the 1967 graduating class was unemployed.

Mayor Cavanagh had appointed many Negroes to key positions in his administration, but in elective offices the Negro population was still under-represented. Of nine councilmen, one was a Negro. Of seven school board members, two were Negroes.

Although federal programs had brought nearly $360 million to the city between 1962 and 1967, the money appeared to have had little impact at the grass roots. Urban renewal, for which $38 million had been allocated, was opposed by many residents of the poverty areas.

Because of its financial straits, the city was unable to produce on promises to correct such conditions as poor garbage collection and bad street lighting, which brought constant complaints from Negro residents.

On 12th Street Carl Perry, the Negro proprietor of a drug store and photography studio, was dispensing ice cream, sodas, and candy to the youngsters streaming in and out of his store. For safekeeping he had brought the photography equipment from his studio, in the next block, to the drug store. The youths milling about repeatedly assured him that, although the market next door had been ransacked, his place of business was in no danger.

In mid-afternoon the market was set afire. Soon after, the drug store went up in flames.

State Representative James Del Rio, a Negro, was camping out in front of a building he owned when two small boys, neither more than 10 years old, approached. One prepared to throw a brick through the window. Del Rio stopped him: "That building belongs to me," he said.

"I'm glad you told me, baby, because I was just about to bust you in!" the youngster replied.

Some evidence that criminal elements were organizing spontaneously to take advantage of the riot began to manifest itself. A number of cars were noted to be returning again and again, their occupants methodically looting stores. Months later, goods stolen during the riot were still being peddled.

A spirit of carefree nihilism was taking hold. To riot and to destroy appeared more and more to become ends in themselves. Late Sunday afternoon it appeared to one observer that the young people were "dancing amidst the flames."

A Negro plainclothes officer was standing at an intersection when a man threw a Molotov cocktail into a business establishment at the corner. In the heat of the afternoon, fanned by the 20 to 25 m.p.h. winds of both Sunday and Monday, the fire reached the home next door within minutes. As residents uselessly sprayed the flames with garden hoses, the fire jumped from roof to roof of adjacent two- and three-story buildings. Within the hour the entire block was in flames. The ninth house in the burning row belonged to the arsonist who had thrown the Molotov cocktail.

In some areas residents organized rifle squads to protect firefighters. Elsewhere, especially as the wind-whipped flames began to overwhelm the Detroit Fire Department and more and more residences burned, the firemen were subjected to curses and rock-throwing.

Because of a lack of funds, on a per capita basis the department is one of the smallest in the nation—in comparison to Newark, where approximately 1,000 firemen must cover a city of 140 square miles with a population of 1.6 million. Because the department had no mutual aid agreement with surrounding communities, it could not quickly call in reinforcements from outlying areas, and it was almost 9:00 P.M. before the first arrived. At one point, out of a total of 92 pieces of Detroit fire-fighting equipment and 56 brought in from surrounding communities, only four engine companies were available to guard areas of the city outside of the riot perimeter.

As the afternoon progressed, the fire department's radio carried repeated messages of apprehension and orders of caution:

There is no police protection here at all; there isn't a policeman in the area. . . . If you have any trouble at all, pull out! . . . We're being stoned at the scene. It's going good. We need help! . . . Protect yourselves! Proceed away from the scene. . . . Engine 42 over at Linwood and Gladstone. They are throwing bottles at us so we are getting out of the area. . . . All companies without police protection—all companies without police protection—orders are to withdraw, do not try to put out the fires. I repeat—all companies without police protection orders are to withdraw, do not try to put out the fires!

It was 4:30 P.M. when the firemen, some of them exhausted by the heat, abandoned an area of approximately 100 square blocks on either side of 12th Street to await protection from police and National Guardsmen.

During the course of the riot firemen were to withdraw 283 times.

Fire Chief Charles J. Quinlan estimated that at least two-thirds of the buildings were destroyed by spreading fires rather than fires set at the scene. Of the 683 structures involved, approximately one-third were residential, and in few, if any, of these was the fire set originally.

Governor George Romney flew over the area between 8:30 and 9:00 P.M. "It looked like the city had been bombed on the west side and there was an area two-and-a-half miles by three-and-a-half miles with major fires, with entire blocks in flames," he told the Commission.

In the midst of chaos there were some unexpected individual responses.

Twenty-four-year-old E. G., a Negro born in Savannah, Georgia, had come to Detroit in 1965 to attend Wayne State University. Rebellion had been building in him for a long time because,

You just had to bow down to the white man. . . . When the insurance man would come by he would always call out to my mother by her first name, and we were expected to smile and greet him happily . . . Man, I know he would never have thought of me or my father going to his house and calling his wife by her first name. Then I once saw a white man slapping a young pregnant Negro woman on the street with such force that she just spun around and fell. I'll never forget that.

When a friend called to tell him about the riot on 12th Street, E. G. went there expecting "a true revolt," but was disappointed as soon as he saw the looting begin: "I wanted to see the people really rise up in revolt. When I saw the first person coming out of the store with things in his arms, I really got sick to my stomach and wanted to go home. Rebellion against the white suppressors is one thing, but one measly pair of shoes or some food completely ruins the whole concept."

E. G. was standing in a crowd, watching firemen work, when Fire Chief Alvin Wall called out for help from the spectators. E. G. responded. His reasoning was: "No matter what color someone is, whether they are green or pink or blue, I'd help them if they were in trouble. That's all there is to it."

He worked with the firemen for four days, the only Negro in an all-white crew. Elsewhere, at scattered locations, a half dozen other Negro youths pitched in to help the firemen.

At 4:20 P.M. Mayor Cavanagh requested that the National Guard be brought into Detroit, although a major portion of several hundred troops were conducting their regular weekend drill in the city. That circumstance obviated many problems. The first troops were on the streets by 7:00 P.M.

At 7:45 P.M. the mayor issued a proclamation instituting a 9:00 P.M. to 5:00 A.M. curfew. At 9:07 P.M. the first sniper fire was reported. Following his aerial survey of the city, Governor Romney, at or shortly before midnight, proclaimed that "a state of public emergency exists" in the cities of Detroit, Highland Park, and Hamtramck.

At 4:45 P.M. a 68-year-old white shoe-repairman, George Messerlian, had seen looters carrying clothes from a cleaning establishment next to his shop. Armed with a saber, he had rushed into the street, flailing away at the looters. One Negro youth was nicked on the shoulder. Another, who had not been on the scene, inquired as to what had happened. After he had been told, he allegedly replied: "I'll get the old man for you!"

Going up to Messerlian, who had fallen or been knocked to the ground, the youth began to beat him with a club. Two other Negro youths dragged the attacker away from the old man. It was too late. Messerlian died four days later in the hospital.

At 9:15 P.M. a 16-year-old Negro boy, superficially wounded while looting, became the first reported gunshot victim.

At midnight Sharon George, a 23-year-old white woman, together with her two brothers, was a passenger in a car being driven by her husband. After having dropped off two Negro friends, they were returning home on one of Detroit's main avenues when they were slowed by a milling throng in the street. A shot fired from close range struck the car. The bullet splintered in Mrs. George's body. She died less than two hours later.

An hour before midnight a 45-year-old white man, Walter Grzanka, together with three white companions, went into the street. Shortly thereafter a market was broken into. Inside the show window a Negro man began filling bags with groceries and handing them to confederates outside the store. Grzanka twice went over to the store, accepted bags, and placed them down beside his companions across the street. On the third occasion he entered the market. When he emerged, the market owner, driving by in his car, shot and killed him.

In Grzanka's pockets police found seven cigars, four packages of pipe tobacco, and nine pairs of shoelaces.

Before dawn four other looters were shot, one of them accidentally while struggling with a police officer. A Negro youth and a National Guardsman were injured by gunshots of undetermined origin. A private guard shot himself while pulling his revolver from his pocket. In the basement of the 13th Precinct Police Station a cue ball, thrown by an unknown assailant, cracked against the head of a sergeant.

At about midnight three white youths, armed with a shotgun, had gone to the roof of their apartment building, located in an all-white block, in order, they said, to protect the building from fire. At 2:45 A.M. a patrol car, carrying police officers and National Guardsmen, received a report of "snipers on the roof." As the patrol car arrived, the manager of the building went to the roof to tell the youths they had better come down.

The law enforcement personnel surrounded the building, some going to the front, others to the rear. As the manager, together with the three youths, descended the fire escape in the rear, a National Guardsman, believing he heard shots from the front, fired. His shot killed 23-year-old Clifton Pryor.

Early in the morning a young white fireman and a 49-year-old Negro homeowner were killed by fallen power lines.

By 2:00 A.M. Monday, Detroit police had been augmented by 800 State Police officers and 1,200 National Guardsmen. An additional 8,000 Guardsmen were on the way. Nevertheless, Governor Romney and Mayor Cavanagh decided to ask for federal assistance. At 2:15 A.M. the mayor called Vice President Hubert Humphrey, and was referred to Attorney General Ramsey Clark. A short time thereafter telephone contact was established between Governor Romney and the attorney general.

There is some difference of opinion about what occurred next. According to Attorney General Ramsey Clark's office, the governor was advised of the seriousness of the request and told that the applicable federal statute required that, before federal troops could be brought into the city, he would have to state that the situation had deteriorated to the point that local and state forces could no longer maintain law and order. According to the governor, he was under the impression that he was being asked to declare that a "state of insurrection" existed in the city.

The governor was unwilling to make such a declaration, contending that, if he did, insurance policies would not cover the loss incurred as a result of the riot. He and the mayor decided to re-evaluate the need for federal troops.

Contact between Detroit and Washington was maintained throughout the early morning hours. At 9:00 A.M., as the disorder still showed no sign of abating, the governor and the mayor decided to make a renewed request for federal troops.

Shortly before noon the President of the United States authorized the sending of a task force of paratroopers to Selfridge Air Force Base, near the city. A few minutes past 3:00 P.M., Lt. General John L. Throckmorton, commander of Task Force Detroit, met Cyrus Vance, former Deputy Secretary of Defense, at the air base. Approximately an hour later the first federal troops arrived at the air base.

After meeting with state and municipal officials, Mr. Vance, General Throckmorton, Governor Romney, and Mayor Cavanagh made a tour of the city, which lasted until 7:15 P.M. During this tour Mr. Vance and General Throckmorton independently came to the conclusion that—since they had seen no looting or sniping, since the fires appeared to be coming under control, and since a substantial number of National Guardsmen had not yet been committed—injection of federal troops would be premature.

As the riot alternately waxed and waned, one area of the ghetto remained insulated. On the northeast side the residents of some 150 square blocks inhabited by 21,000 persons had, in 1966, banded together in the Positive Neighborhood Action Committee (PNAC). With professional help from the Institute of Urban Dynamics, they had organized block clubs and made plans for the improvement of the neighborhood. In order to meet the need for recreational facilities, which the city was not providing, they had raised $3,000 to purchase empty lots for playgrounds. Although opposed to urban renewal, they had agreed to co-sponsor with the Archdiocese of Detroit a housing project to be controlled jointly by the archdiocese and PNAC.

When the riot broke out, the residents, through the block clubs, were able to organize quickly. Youngsters, agreeing to stay in the neighborhood, participated in detouring traffic. While many persons reportedly sympathized with the idea of a rebellion against the "system," only two small fires were set —one in an empty building.

During the daylight hours Monday, nine more persons were killed by gunshots elsewhere in the city, and many others were seriously or critically injured. Twenty-three-year-old Nathaniel Edmonds, a Negro, was sitting in his back yard when a young white man stopped his car, got out, and began an argument with him. A few minutes later, declaring that he was "going to paint his picture on him with a shotgun," the white man allegedly shot-gunned Edmonds to death.

Mrs. Nannie Pack and Mrs. Mattie Thomas were sitting on the porch of Mrs. Pack's house when police began chasing looters from a nearby market. During the chase officers fired three shots from their shotguns. The discharge from one of these accidentally struck the two women. Both were still in the hospital weeks later.

Included among those critically injured when they were accidentally trapped in the line of fire were an 8-year-old Negro girl and a 14-year-old white boy.

As darkness settled Monday, the number of incidents reported to police began to rise again. Although many turned out to be false, several involved injuries to police officers, National Guardsmen, and civilians by gunshots of undetermined origin.

Watching the upward trend of reported incidents, Mr. Vance and General Throckmorton became convinced federal troops should be used, and President Johnson was so advised. At 11:20 P.M. the President signed a proclamation federalizing the Michigan National Guard and authorizing the use of the paratroopers.

At this time there were nearly 5,000 Guardsmen in the city, but fatigue, lack of training, and the haste with which they had to be deployed reduced their effectiveness. Some of the Guardsmen traveled 200 miles and then were on duty for 30 hours straight. Some had never received riot training and were given on-the-spot instructions on mob control—only to discover that there were no mobs, and that the situation they faced on the darkened streets was one for which they were unprepared.

Commanders committed men as they became available, often in small groups. In the resulting confusion, some units were lost in the city. Two Guardsmen assigned to an intersection on Monday were discovered still there on Friday.

Lessons learned by the California National Guard two years earlier in Watts regarding the danger of overreaction and the necessity of great restraint in using weapons had not, apparently, been passed on to the Michigan National Guard. The young troopers could not be expected to know what a danger they were creating by the lack of fire discipline, not only to the civilian population but to themselves.

A Detroit newspaper reporter who spent a night riding in a command jeep told a Commission investigator of machine guns being fired accidentally, street lights being shot out by rifle fire, and buildings being placed under seige on the sketchiest reports of sniping. Troopers would fire, and immediately from the distance there would be answering fire, sometimes consisting of tracer bullets.

In one instance, the newsman related, a report was received on the jeep radio that an Army bus was pinned down by sniper fire at an intersection. National Guardsmen and police, arriving from various directions, jumped out and began asking each other: "Where's the sniper fire coming from?" As one Guardsman pointed to a building, everyone rushed about, taking cover. A soldier, alighting from a jeep, accidentally pulled the trigger on his rifle. As the shot reverberated through the darkness an officer yelled: "What's going on?" "I don't know," came the answer. "Sniper I guess."

Without any clear authorization or direction someone opened fire upon the suspected building. A tank rolled up and sprayed the building with .50-caliber tracer bullets. Law enforcement officers rushed into the surrounded building and discovered it empty. "They must be firing one shot and running," was the verdict.

The reporter interviewed the men who had gotten off the bus and were crouched around it. When he asked them about the sniping incident he was told that someone had heard a shot. He asked, "Did the bullet hit the bus?" The answer was: "Well, we don't know."

Bracketing the hour of midnight Monday, heavy firing, injuring many persons and killing several, occurred in the southeastern sector, which was to be taken over by the paratroopers at 4:00 A.M. Tuesday, and which was, at this time, considered to be the most active riot area in the city.

Employed as a private guard, 55-year-old Julius L. Dorsey, a Negro, was standing in front of a market when accosted by two Negro men and a woman. They demanded he permit them to loot the market. He ignored their demands. They began to berate him. He asked a neighbor to call the police. As the argument grew more heated, Dorsey fired three shots from his pistol into the air.

The police radio reported: "Looters, they have rifles." A patrol car driven by a police officer and carrying three National Guardsmen arrived. As the looters fled, the law enforcement personnal opened fire. When the firing ceased, one person lay dead.

He was Julius L. Dorsey.

In two areas—one consisting of a triangle formed by Mack, Gratiot, and E. Grand Boulevard, the other surrounding Southeastern High School—firing began shortly after 10:00 P.M. and continued for several hours.

In the first of the areas, a 22-year-old Negro complained that he had been shot at by snipers. Later, a half dozen civilians and one National Guardsman were wounded by shots of undetermined origin.

Henry Denson, a passenger in a car, was shot and killed when the vehicle's driver, either by accident or intent, failed to heed a warning to halt at a National Guard roadblock.

Similar incidents occurred in the vicinity of Southeastern High School, one of the National Guard staging areas. As early as 10:20 P.M. the area was reported to be under sniper fire. Around midnight there were two incidents, the sequence of which remains in doubt.

Shortly before midnight Ronald Powell, who lived three blocks east of the high school and whose wife was, momentarily, expecting a baby, asked the four friends with whom he had been spending the evening to take him home. He, together with Edward Blackshear, Charles Glover, and John Leroy, climbed into Charles Dunson's station wagon for the short drive. Some of the five may have been drinking, but none was intoxicated.

To the north of the high school they were halted at a National Guard roadblock, and told they would have to detour around the school and a fire station at Mack and St. Jean Streets because of the firing that had been occurring. Following orders, they took a circuitous route and approached Powell's home from the south.

On Lycaste Street, between Charlevoix and Goethe, they saw a jeep sitting at the curb. Believing it to be another roadblock, they slowed down. Simultaneously a shot rang out. A National Guardsman fell, hit in the ankle.

Other National Guardsmen at the scene thought the shot had come from the station wagon. Shot after shot was directed against the vehicle, at least 17 of them finding their mark. All five occupants were injured, John Leroy fatally.

At approximately the same time firemen, police, and National Guardsmen at the corner of Mack and St. Jean Streets, two and one-half blocks away, again came under fire from what they believed were rooftop snipers to the southeast, the direction of Charlevoix and Lycaste. The police and Guardsmen responded with a hail of fire.

When the shooting ceased, Carl Smith, a young firefighter, lay dead. An autopsy determined that the shot had been fired at street level, and, according to police, probably had come from the southeast.

At 4:00 A.M. when paratroopers, under the command of Col. A. R. Bolling, arrived at the high school, the area was so dark and still that the colonel thought, at first, that he had come to the wrong place. Investigating, he discovered National Guard troops, claiming they were pinned down by sniper fire, crouched behind the walls of the darkened building.

The colonel immediately ordered all the lights in the building turned on and his troops to show themselves as conspicuously as possible. In the apartment house across the street nearly every window had been shot out, and the walls were pockmarked with bullet holes. The colonel went into the building and began talking to the residents, many of whom had spent the night huddled on the floor. He reassured them no more shots would be fired.

According to Lt. Gen. Throckmorton and Colonel Bolling, the city, at this time, was saturated with fear. The National Guardsmen were afraid, the residents were afraid, and the police were afraid. Numerous persons, the majority of them Negroes, were being injured by gunshots of undetermined origin. The general and his staff felt that the major task of the troops was to reduce the fear and restore an air of normalcy.

In order to accomplish this, every effort was made to establish contact and rapport between the troops and the residents. Troopers—20 percent of whom were Negro—began helping to clean up the streets, collect garbage, and trace persons who had disappeared in the confusion. Residents in the neighborhoods responded with soup and sandwiches for the troops. In areas where the National Guard tried to establish rapport with the citizens, there was a similar response.*

---

*EDITOR'S NOTE: In a "Summary of (the Kerner) Report" (1968) published by 23 organizations—including the American Jewish Committee, the National Catholic Conference for Interracial Justice, the National Council of Churches, the A. Philip Randolph Institute, and the United Auto Workers—the term "similar" was noted as "smaller" in the statement (p. 5) ". . . where the National Guard tried to establish rapport with the citizens, there was a *smaller* response." (editor's emphasis) From what this observer saw in the riot area the summary report version is more accurate.

Within hours after the arrival of the paratroops the area occupied by them was the quietest in the city, bearing out General Throckmorton's view that the key to quelling a disorder is to saturate an area with "calm, determined, and hardened professional soldiers." Loaded weapons, he believes, are unnecessary. Troopers had strict orders not to fire unless they could see the specific person at whom they were aiming. Mass fire was forbidden.

During five days in the city, 2,700 Army troops expended only 201 rounds of ammunition, almost all during the first few hours, after which even stricter fire discipline was enforced. (In contrast, New Jersey National Guardsmen and State police expended 13,326 rounds of ammunition in the three days in Newark.) Hundreds of reports of sniper fire—most of them false—continued to pour into police headquarters; the Army logged only 10. No paratrooper was injured by a gunshot. Only one person was hit by a shot fired by a trooper. He was a young Negro who was killed when he ran into the line of fire as a trooper, aiding police in a raid on an apartment, aimed at a person believed to be a sniper.

General Throckmorton ordered the weapons of all military personnel unloaded, but either the order failed to reach many National Guardsmen, or else it was disobeyed.

Even as the general was requesting the city to relight the streets, Guardsmen continued shooting out the lights, and there are reports of dozens of shots being fired to dispatch one light. At one such location, as Guardsmen were shooting out the street lights, a radio newscaster reported himself to be pinned down by "sniper fire."

On the same day that the general was attempting to restore normalcy by ordering street barricades taken down, Guardsmen on one street were not only, in broad daylight, ordering people off the street, but off their porches and away from the windows. Two persons who failed to respond to the order quickly enough were shot, one of them fatally.

The general himself reported an incident of a Guardsman "firing across the bow" of an automobile that was approaching a roadblock.

As in Los Angeles two years earlier, roadblocks that were ill-lighted and ill-defined—often consisting of no more than a trash barrel or similar object with Guardsmen standing nearby—proved a continuous hazard to motorists. At one such roadblock, National Guard Sergeant Larry Post, standing in the street, was caught in a sudden cross fire as his fellow Guardsmen opened up on a vehicle. He was the only soldier killed in the riot.

With persons of every description arming themselves, and guns being fired accidentally or on the vaguest pretext all over the city, it became more and more impossible to tell who was shooting at whom. Some firemen began carrying guns. One accidentally shot and wounded a fellow fireman. Another injured himself.

The chaos of a riot, and the difficulties faced by police officers, are demonstrated by an incident that occurred at 2:00 A.M. Tuesday.

A unit of 12 officers received a call to guard firemen from snipers. When they arrived at the corner of Vicksburg and Linwood in the 12th Street area, the intersection was well-lighted by the flames completely enveloping one building. Sniper fire was directed at the officers from an alley to the north, and gun flashes were observed in two buildings.

As the officers advanced on the two buildings, Patrolman Johnie [*sic*] Hamilton fired several rounds from his machine gun. Thereupon, the officers were suddenly subjected to fire from a new direction, the east. Hamilton, struck by four bullets, fell, critically injured, in the intersection. As two officers ran to his aid, they too were hit.

By this time other units of the Detroit Police Department, state police, and National Guard had arrived on the scene, and the area was covered with a hail of gunfire.

In the confusion the snipers who had initiated the shooting escaped.

At 9:15 P.M. Tuesday, July 25, 38-year-old Jack Sydnor, a Negro, came home drunk. Taking out his pistol, he fired one shot into an alley. A few minutes later the police arrived. As his common-law wife took refuge in a closet, Sydnor waited, gun in hand, while the police forced open the door. Patrolman Roger Poike, the first to enter, was shot by Sydnor. Although critically injured, the officer managed to get off six shots in return. Police within the building and on the street then poured a hail of fire into the apartment. When the shooting ceased, Sydnor's body, riddled by gunfire, was found lying on the ground outside a window.

Nearby, a state police officer and a Negro youth were struck and seriously injured by stray bullets. As in other cases where the origin of the shots was not immediately determinable, police reported them as "shot by sniper."

Reports of "heavy sniper fire" poured into police headquarters from the two blocks surrounding the apartment house where the battle with Jack Sydnor had taken place. National Guard troops with two tanks were dispatched to help flush out the snipers.

Shots continued to be heard throughout the neighborhood. At approximately midnight—there are discrepancies as to the precise time—a machine gunner on a tank, startled by several shots, asked the assistant gunner where the shots were coming from. The assistant gunner pointed toward a flash in the window of an apartment house from which there had been earlier reports of sniping.

The machine gunner opened fire. As the slugs ripped through the window and walls of the apartment, they nearly severed the arm of 21-year-old Valerie Hood. Her 4-year-old niece, Tonya Blanding, toppled dead, a .50-caliber bullet hole in her chest.

A few seconds earlier, 19-year-old Bill Hood, standing in the window, had lighted a cigarette.

Down the street, a bystander was critically injured by a stray bullet. Simultaneously, the John C. Lodge Freeway, two blocks away, was reported to be under sniper fire. Tanks and National Guard troops were sent to investigate. At the Harlan House Motel, ten blocks from where Tonya Blanding had died a short time earlier, Mrs. Helen Hall, a 51-year-old white businesswoman, opened the drapes of the fourth floor hall window. Calling out to other guests, she exclaimed: "Look at the tanks!"

She died seconds later as bullets began to slam into the building. As the firing ceased, a 19-year-old Marine Pfc., carrying a Springfield rifle, burst into the building. When, accidentally, he pushed the rifle barrel through a window, the firing commenced anew. A police investigation showed that the Marine, who had just decided to "help out" the law enforcement personnel, was not involved in the death of Mrs. Hall.

R.R., a white 27-year-old coin dealer, was the owner of an expensive, three-story house on "L" Street, an integrated middle-class neighborhood. In May of 1966, he and his wife and child had moved to New York and had rented the house to two young men. After several months he had begun to have problems with his tenants. On one occasion he reported to his attorney that he had been threatened by them.

In March of 1967, R.R. instituted eviction proceedings. These were still pending when the riot broke out. Concerned about the house, R.R. decided to fly to Detroit. When he arrived at the house, on Wednesday, July 26, he discovered the tenants were not at home.

He then called his attorney, who advised him to take physical possession of the house and, for legal purposes, to take witnesses along.

Together with his 17-year-old brother and another white youth, R.R. went to the house, entered, and began changing the locks on the doors. For protection they brought a .22 caliber rifle, which R.R.'s brother took into the cellar and fired into a pillow in order to test it.

Shortly after 8:00 P.M., R.R. called his attorney to advise him that the tenants had returned, and he had refused to admit them. Thereupon, R.R. alleged, the tenants had threatened to obtain the help of the National Guard. The attorney relates that he was not particularly concerned. He told R.R. that if the National Guard did appear he should have the officer in charge call him (the attorney).

At approximately the same time the National Guard claims it received information to the effect that several men had evicted the legal occupants of the house, and intended to start sniping after dark.

A National Guard column was dispatched to the scene. Shortly after 9:00 P.M., in the half-light of dusk, the column of approximately 30 men surrounded the house. A tank took position on a lawn across the street. The captain commanding the column placed in front of the house an explosive device similar to a firecracker. After setting this off in order to draw the attention of the occupants to the presence of the column, he called for them to come out of the house. No attempt was made to verify the truth or false-hood of the allegations regarding snipers.

When the captain received no reply from the house, he began counting to 10. As he was counting, he said, he heard another shot and saw a "fire streak" coming from an upstairs window. He thereupon gave the order to fire.

According to the three young men, they were on the second floor of the house and completely bewildered by the barrage of fire that was unleashed against it. As hundreds of bullets crashed through the first and second-story windows and ricocheted off the walls, they dashed to the third floor. Pro-tected by a large chimney, they huddled in a closet until, during a lull in the firing, they were able to wave an item of clothing out of the window as a sign of surrender. They were arrested as snipers.

The firing from rifles and machine guns had been so intense that in a period of a few minutes it inflicted an estimated $10,000 worth of damage. One of a pair of stone columns was shot nearly in half.

Jailed at the 10th Precinct Station sometime Wednesday night R.R. and his two companions were taken from their cell to an "alley court," police slang for an unlawful attempt to make prisoners confess. A police officer, who has resigned from the force, allegedly administered such a severe beating to R.R. that the bruises still were visible two weeks later.

R.R.'s 17-year-old brother had his skull cracked open, and was thrown back into the cell. He was taken to a hospital only when other arrestees com-plained that he was bleeding to death.

At the preliminary hearing 12 days later the prosecution presented only one witness, the National Guard captain who had given the order to fire. The police officer who had signed the original complaint was not asked to take the stand. The charges against all three of the young men were dismissed.

Nevertheless, the morning after the original incident, a major metro-politan newspaper in another section of the country composed the following banner story from wire service reports:

DETROIT, July 27 (Thursday)—Two National Guard tanks ripped a sniper's haven with machine guns Wednesday night and flushed out three shaggy-haired white youths. Snipers attacked a guard command post and Detroit's racial riot set a modern record for bloodshed. The death toll soared to 36, topping the Watts bloodbath of 1966 in which 35 died and making Detroit's insurrection the most deadly racial riot in modern U.S. history. . . .

In the attack on the sniper's nest, the Guardsmen poured hundreds of rounds of .50 caliber machine gun fire into the home, which authorities said housed arms and ammunition used by West Side sniper squads.

Guardsmen recovered guns and ammunition. A reporter with the troopers said the house, a neat brick home in a neighborhood of $20,000 to $50,000 homes, was torn apart by the machine gun and rifle fire.

Sniper fire crackled from the home as the Guard unit approached. It was one of the first verified reports of sniping by whites.   .   .   .

A pile of loot taken from riot-ruined stores was recovered from the sniper's haven, located ten blocks from the heart of the 200-square-block riot zone.

Guardsmen said the house had been identified as a storehouse of arms and ammunition for snipers. Its arsenal was regarded as an indication that the sniping —or at least some of it—was organized.

As hundreds of arrestees were brought into the 10th Precinct Station, officers took it upon themselves to carry on investigations and to attempt to extract confessions. Dozens of charges of police brutality emanated from the station as prisoners were brought in uninjured, but later had to be taken to the hospital.

In the absence of the precinct commander, who had transferred his headquarters to the riot command post at a nearby hospital, discipline vanished. Prisoners who requested that they be permitted to notify someone of their arrest were almost invariably told that: "The telephones are out of order." Congressman Conyers and State Representative Del Rio, who went to the station hoping to coordinate with the police the establishing of a community patrol, were so upset by what they saw that they changed their minds and gave up on the project.

A young woman, brought into the station, was told to strip. After she had done so, and while an officer took pictures with a Polaroid camera, another officer came up to her and began fondling her. The negative of one of the pictures, fished out of a waste basket, subsequently was turned over to the mayor's office.

Citing the sniper danger, officers throughout the department had taken off their bright metal badges. They also had taped over the license plates and the numbers of the police cars. Identification of individual officers became virtually impossible.

On a number of occasions officers fired at fleeing looters, then made little attempt to determine whether their shots had hit anyone. Later some of the persons were discovered dead or injured in the street.

In one such case police and National Guardsmen were interrogating a youth suspected of arson when, according to officers, he attempted to escape. As he vaulted over the hood of an automobile, an officer fired his shotgun. The youth disappeared on the other side of the car. Without making an investigation, the officers and Guardsmen returned to their car and drove off.

When nearby residents called police, another squad car arrived to pick up the body. Despite the fact that an autopsy disclosed the youth had been killed by five shotgun pellets, only a cursory investigation was made, and the death was attributed to "sniper fire." No police officer at the scene during the shooting filed a report.

Not until a Detroit newspaper editor presented to the police the statements of several witnesses claiming that the youth had been shot by police after he had been told to run did the department launch an investigation. Not until three weeks after the shooting did an officer come forward to identify himself as the one who had fired the fatal shot.

Citing conflicts in the testimony of the score of witnesses, the Detroit Prosecutor's office declined to press charges.

Prosecution is proceeding in the case of three youths in whose shotgun deaths law enforcement personnel were implicated following a report that snipers were firing from the Algiers Motel. In fact, there is little evidence that anyone fired from inside the building. Two witnesses say that they had seen a man, standing outside of the motel, fire two shots from a rifle. The interrogation of other persons revealed that law enforcement personnel then shot out one or more street lights. Police patrols responded to the shots. An attack was launched on the motel.

The picture is further complicated by the fact that this incident occurred at roughly the same time that the National Guard was directing fire at the apartment house in which Tonya Blanding was killed. The apartment house was only six blocks distant from and in a direct line with the motel.

The killings occurred when officers began on-the-spot questioning of the occupants of the motel in an effort to discover weapons used in the "sniping." Several of those questioned reportedly were beaten. One was a Negro ex-paratrooper who had only recently been honorably discharged, and had gone to Detroit to look for a job.

Although by late Tuesday looting and fire-bombing had virtually ceased, between 7:00 and 11:00 P.M., that night there were 444 reports of incidents. Most were reports of sniper fire.

During the daylight hours of July 26th, there were 534 such reports. Between 8:30 and 11:00 P.M. there were 255. As they proliferated, the pressure on law enforcement officers to uncover the snipers became intense. Homes were broken into. Searches were made on the flimsiest of tips. A Detroit newspaper headline aptly proclaimed: "Everyone's Suspect in No Man's Land."

Before the arrest of a young woman IBM operator in the city assessor's office brought attention to the situation on Friday, July 28th, any person with a gun in his home was liable to be picked up as a suspect.

Of the 27 persons charged with sniping, 22 had charges against them dismissed at preliminary hearings, and the charges against two others were dismissed later. One pleaded guilty to possession of an unregistered gun and was given a suspended sentence. Trials of two are pending.

In all, more than 7,200 persons were arrested. Almost 3,000 of these were picked up on the second day of the riot, and by midnight Monday 4,000 were incarcerated in makeshift jails. Some were kept as long as 30 hours on buses. Others spent days in an underground garage without toilet facilities. An uncounted number were people who had merely been unfortunate enough to be on the wrong street at the wrong time. Included were members of the press whose attempts to show their credentials had been ignored. Released later, they were chided for not having exhibited their identification at the time of their arrests.

The booking system proved incapable of adequately handling the large number of arrestees. People became lost for days in the maze of different detention facilities. Until the later stages, bail was set deliberately high, often at $10,000 or more. When it became apparent that this policy was unrealistic and unworkable, the Prosecutor's office began releasing on low bail or on their own recognizance hundreds of those who had been picked up. Nevertheless, this fact was not publicized for fear of antagonizing those who had demanded a high-bail policy.

Of the 43 persons who were killed during the riot, 33 were Negro and 10 were white. Fifteen citizens (of whom four were white), one white National Guardsman, one white fireman, and one Negro private guard died as the result of gunshot wounds. Most of these deaths appear to have been accidental, but criminal homicide is suspected in some.

Two persons, including one fireman, died as a result of fallen power lines. Two were burned to death. One was a drunken gunman; one an arson suspect. One white man was killed by a rioter. One police officer was felled by a shotgun blast when his gun, in the hands of another officer, accidentally discharged during a scuffle with a looter.

Action by police officers accounted for 20 and, very likely, 21 of the deaths. Action by the National Guard for seven, and, very likely, nine; action by the Army for one. Two deaths were the result of action by store owners. Four persons died accidentally. Rioters were responsible for two, and perhaps three of the deaths; a private guard for one. A white man is suspected of murdering a Negro youth. The perpetrator of one of the killings in the Algiers Motel remains unknown.

Damage estimates, originally set as high as $500 million, were quickly scaled down. The city assessor's office placed the loss—excluding business stock, private furnishings, and the buildings of churches and charitable institutions—at approximately $22 million. Insurance payments, according to the State Insurance Bureau, will come to about $32 million, representing an estimated 65 to 75 percent of the total loss.

By Thursday, July 27, most riot activity had ended. The paratroopers were removed from the city on Saturday. On Tuesday, August 1, the curfew was lifted and the National Guard moved out.

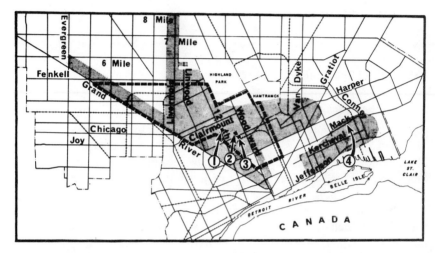

Map of Riot Area. Shown on the map in shaded areas are the places where looting and arson occurred. The numbered areas point to the scenes of major sniper battles (*The Detroit News,* Friday, August 11, 1967).

Profile of the Riot Causes
and Participants

Robert A. Mendelsohn

The research to be presented here is the result of many influences. That is to say, the techniques used for investigation, the people interviewed, and the kinds of questions asked are the results of many interplaying forces. Some came from hypotheses about the situation of the Negro in the United States. Some came from knowledge of psychological motivation. Other influences were hypotheses derived from previous research on riots and other mass movements. Additionally, practical matters influenced the form of the study. These included the availability of materials from other research done on recent urban riots,[1] practicalities of time and personnel. The goal of the study has been to contribute to knowledge of race relations, of the Negro subculture, of the dynamics of riots. Specifically, in regard to the riot in Detroit, the goals were to determine who participated in it and why; what whites and Negroes felt caused the riot; what portents there are about the future; and what whites and Negroes see as the current status and future of race relations.

To understand a riot and the research that emanates from it requires a discussion of a variety of topics. Accordingly, the opening section of the paper will discuss the causes of riots, with the analysis centering on the recent racially related riots. Following this will be a discussion of the research design of the study done in Detroit. Finally, the key empirical findings of that study will be summarized.

The author is on the research faculty of the Lafayette Clinic, Wayne State University. This paper is a modification and extension of an address originally presented at the Conference of Religious and Lay Leaders, Detroit, Michigan, September 22, 1967. The research was supported by a grant from the National Institute of Mental Health. This article is previously unpublished.
1. Of particular value were the interview schedules made available to the study by the Los Angeles Riot Study, Dr. Nathan Cohen, Coordinator.

70

The Causes of Urban Riots

When a striking, frightening, dramatic, and socially upsetting event such as befell the City of Detroit in July, 1967, occurs, there is a strong temptation to treat it as an isolated, discrete event; to concentrate on those aspects of the event which are dramatic and frightening and avoid discussion of causes; to explain it as one of those pathological events that periodically seem to afflict mankind but which are outside the ordinary flow of history; or to see the fault as lying in the character of the perpetrators or the nature of human beings in general. These are failures of imagination stemming both from educational deficiencies and from the emotional need to reject explanations that reveal the true nature of the event due to the discomfort that would follow. It seems reassuring to deny that this outburst is symptomatic of a general malaise. This is a gross error. The causes of Detroit's riot are complex but clearly rooted in ancient and current wrongs, current anxieties and conditions, and the dynamics of group psychology. The riot is in fact a climax of many causes which in turn point to a major social crisis. Let me specify some of these background causes of the wave of urban riots.

First is the general character of Negro-white relations in the United States and in Detroit specifically. It is clear that race relations have been, and remain, of a predominantly negative character and that racism continues. There have been, to be sure, important changes, but these changes have done little to remove the basic grievances of the Negro American nor have they eliminated the social and economic injustices that continue to assail him. In fact, as will be discussed below, the positive changes themselves make a substantial contribution to social unrest. Thus, if it is true that for many Negroes opportunities never before available are open, it is equally true that for a large group, life in White America goes on very much as before. Indeed it is probable that life for the unskilled lower-class Negro is *relatively* worse than before. Even for the middle-class Negro things are far from acceptable. He cannot live in many sections of the State of Michigan and must continue to put up with subtle and not so subtle insults and bars because of his color. Despite having done all the things he was supposed to have done, and succeeded, he is often neither a full citizen nor a respected one. Further, in the background always lurks the spectre that such gains are conditional—that no matter how worthy, talented, or "respectable" he is, he may suddenly, given the nature of white society, find himself transformed from the tentative and unstable category "person who has earned his status" to that of "Negro who is to be feared and degraded." The Negro American is entirely justified in believing that this country is for whites and he is here on their tolerance.

An examination of American society reveals these basic truths. The executives of our great bureaucracies and other power bases, with few exceptions, are white. There is but one Negro Senator in the United States Senate. At every educational level, Negroes earn less than whites and the Negro unemployment rate is twice that of whites and extraordinarily high among youth.[2] Only 4% of college students are Negro,[3] and when predominantly Negro schools are not included in this figure, the percentage is cut almost in half. Furthermore, this represents a substantial gain in the last few years. The percentage of black police officers, with but few exceptions, is a fraction of the size of the black community within those cities.[4] Until recently, the mass media neither employed in news gathering activities, nor portrayed, Negro Americans.[5] The suburbs are overwhelmingly white with the great mass of the Negro population in the North being relegated to the cities, often to the oldest and most decaying parts. But it is hardly necessary to itemize the well-known list of problems and injustices for they are extensively documented in the Kerner Report and elsewhere.

On a superficial glance, Detroit looked different. Indeed, one of the reasons that people did not expect civil disturbances in Detroit was based on a view that Detroit was, of all large American cities, a good place for Negroes to live. After all, did not Detroit have integrated neighborhoods, one of the largest Negro middle classes in America, Negroes in positions of status and authority? Yes, there was some truth to this, but sometimes these facts mean little and often in fact are really evidence for a negative rather than a positive trend. Without discussing all these presumed advantages, an observation or two should suffice. With few exceptions integrated neighborhoods are integrated, not because whites and Negroes find it rewarding to live together, but because Negroes are moving in, whites are moving out and in that process there have to be some whites and Negroes in the neighborhood at a given time. A study done at Eastern Michigan University[6] and completed just before the riot clearly shows that, contrary to popular belief, integration is on the decline in Detroit, not on the increase. This finding re-

2. Report of the National Advisory Commission on Civil Disorders, hereafter called the "Kerner Report," 1968, pp. 251-253.
3. *Newsweek,* February 10, 1969, p. 53.
4. In the five cities with the largest percentage of Negro population (range 39-63%), the percentage of black officers is 4 to 21. In most cities, the percentage of Negro officers is trivial (Kerner Report, p. 321.) Recruiting efforts since the major riots in a number of cities have reduced, but hardly eliminated, this deficiency.
5. As any viewer of TV is aware, changes have occurred within the mass media. Many stations and papers have added black reporters. Negroes appear in ads and on programs, and genuine efforts have been made by some to portray meaningfully the situation and feelings of the Negro. Yet it remains true that the media remains white-dominated and that employment, particularly at higher levels, remains all but closed to Negroes.
6. *Detroit Free Press,* September 10, 1967.

confirmed that of Mayer and Hoult in their Wayne State University study five years earlier. Whites and Negroes are communicating less, not more, and neighborhood segregation is increasing not decreasing. Take another situation. The large Negro middle class looks like a positive feature of the Detroit community and in many respects it is. But this should not blind us to the fact that Detroit is no different from any large American city in its unemployment rate among the young, lower-class Negro male. In summary, the conditions of life for the Negro American are not acceptable anywhere in the United States, regardless of whether the city is considered a disaster like Newark or a "model city" as Detroit was once characterized.

Obviously, the degrading effects of this condition are a source of deep bitterness and are a central cause of riots. Yet even this does not start riots in and of itself. Poverty, discrimination, and disparities between what a man is and how he is perceived and reacted to abound in the life of people anywhere. But the situation for the Negro American is different, for he has heard promises for over one hundred years and has a history of being exploited for three hundred years. We are not working from a fresh starting point any more. His impatience is rational, his anger is justified, and his feelings that normal channels for social change are bankrupt may be closer to reality than we care to acknowledge. But still this does not entirely account for riots and unrest. It is necessary to go further and discuss other causes.

A second background cause of the riots is the creation of a group of angry, young, lower-class Negro males.[7] The internalization of moral codes against aggression, for a number of reasons too complex to go into here in much detail, is a very difficult task in lower-class groups in general,[8] and in the Negro lower class in particular.[9] This, in turn, is compounded by the following social conditions. First, today every man can see what the "good life" is just by turning on his TV set. Second, the most aggressive group in terms of class and age is markedly under-employed. Third, self-respect and attaining manhood are difficult to achieve for members of a stigmatized group while the societally accepted link between aggressive lashing out and manhood seems to offer a valid way to attain that self-respect. Fourth, the rage against whites once suppressed is increasingly finding overt ex-

7. W. H. Grier and P. M. Cobbs, *Black Rage* (New York: Basic Books, 1968). As Grier and Cobbs persuasively argue, most Negroes of all classes are angry. The concern here is with that group most likely to act on that anger.
8. D. Krech, R. S. Crutchfield, and E. L. Ballachey, *Individual in Society* (New York: McGraw-Hill Book Co., Inc., 1962); U. Bronfenbrenner, "Socialization and Social Class Through Time and Space," in *Readings in Social Psychology*, 3rd ed., edited by E. E. MacCoby, T. M. Newcomb, and E. L. Hartley (New York: The Free Press, 1965).
9. T. F. Pettigrew, *A Profile of the Negro American* (Princeton, N.J.: D. Van Nostrand Co., Inc., 1964), chapt. 6.

pression. Fifth, there has been an increasing legitimization of violence.[10] The end result of these conditions and the socialization pattern contains all the makings of social dynamite. The Kerner Report unequivocally reveals that it is the young male who is the most active and destructive in the early stages of a riot and that older people tend not to be greatly involved unless normal social control breaks down. It is precisely this group with whom Negro leaders and city officials have failed to communicate.

Why does such a group, so dangerous to an orderly society, exist? The answer lies in part in history and modern technology. Historically, many Negro families developed along matriarchal lines. Under slavery and the serfdom that followed, the adult male was often separated from his family or his role within the family was invalidated. This left the mother as the stable adult figure in the family and in terms of Western concepts of masculinity, this effectively emasculated many Negro males. Many a male, unable to validate his masculine role and literally trained for passivity (often a necessary defense for survival in a hostile white society), too often proved unreliable to his mate. The Negro female often came to distrust and be contemptuous of the male, leading to a far greater involvement with her daughters than her sons. This, plus the conditions of life in the ghetto, permitted, and in fact often made inevitable, the loss of control by the mother over her sons and at a relatively early age. Studies of how motives for being conventionally successful are taught have demonstrated the great importance that the mother has in teaching her children to strive for success as it is usually defined.[11] Thus we have created a group of males[12] who will not have been socialized, or prepared, to achieve success through acceptable channels, even if opportunity were available, but who nonetheless have the desire to obtain the respect and tangible rewards of a rich society. Furthermore, the absence or perceived impotence of the father makes masculine identification, self-pride, and indeed identity itself more problematic for many Negro males than for his white counterparts. He must spend more energy and time proving his manhood than is the case for those who grow up with an adequately perceived and present father. As I have noted, one way of proving manhood is through aggressive acts, a way which is easily understood and basic to the male stereotype. Fi-

---

10. T. M. Tomlinson and D. O. Sears, "Negro Attitudes Toward the Riot," unpublished paper, Los Angeles Riot Study, 1967. As Tomlinson and Sears have pointed out, riots increasingly have taken on the character of a popular movement, complete with a kind of riot ideology.

11. R. Brown, *Social Psychology* (New York: The Free Press, 1965).

12. Many Negroes through fortunate circumstances or personal qualities escape this outcome despite great obstacles. There is no question that in the past, and increasingly in the present, a strong, vigorous black working and middle class has and continues to evolve. But all too often the conditions described above conspire to entrap young men in the system in numbers sufficient to create the problems under discussion.

nally, the whole tenor of American life, past and present, reinforces aggressive reactions as a way to solve problems. The Negro subgroup is hardly the first group in the United States to resort to violence in the face of deprivation or stigmatization.[13]

Technology and the professionalization of employment practices enter to complete the picture. The introduction of machines to replace manual labor has eliminated a great many of those very jobs that the undertrained Negro youth could do and which gave a start to previous generations of city immigrants. Meanwhile, often irrelevant criteria linked to the growth of the professionalism of employment managers (I.Q. tests, high school diplomas, application forms, etc.) changed the nature of admittance into the job market. The new jobs that technology has created cannot be filled by the undertrained black youth—as Silberman points out 97% of all new jobs are white collar or technical.[14] The energies of the young are released to the street.

A third cause of the riots is that riots seem to work on an instrumental level, at least in the short run. Lipset has noted that groups in power rarely give up any of that power voluntarily but that when they are threatened by the groups below them, they will often make concessions.[15] Riots brought numerous programs to Watts, unprecedented negotiations with the black community over the site and nature of a medical facility in the Newark slums, recreational facilities in Chicago, a black mayor in Cleveland, job programs in Detroit, and so on. As the word gets around that riots work, and little else does, a climate conducive to riots is created.[16] Of course, from an expressive standpoint riots also "work." They undoubtedly release the frustration of years. This "cathartic" effect may help account for the fact that so far in the 1960s a city which has had a major riot has not yet had another.[17] Whether this generalization will continue to hold in the future remains to be seen.

13. H. D. Graham and T. R. Gurr, *Violence in America: Historical and Comparative* (New York: New American Library, 1969).
14. C. E. Silberman, *Crisis in Black and White* (New York: Random House, Inc., 1964).
15. S. M. Lipset, *Political Man* (New York: Doubleday, 1960).
16. It is also true, however, that post-riot changes in programs and the distribution of power may act to reduce the likelihood of riots. For example, in Newark, the inclusion of neighborhood groups in negotiations over the medical center undoubtedly increased the feeling of power and participation of the black community and may have removed some of the root causes of discontent and helped short-circuit a possible future riot.
17. Perhaps a more important reason may be that the experiences in a riot are so disturbing and disruptive that most persons want no part of another, eroding the mass support needed for the development of riot activity. Evidence from Los Angeles (Tomlinson & Sears) and our study in Detroit clearly show that the overwhelming majority of Negroes were markedly negative about the *events* of the riot, even while interpreting the riot as "protest" and often sympathizing with the rioters.

A fourth cause of riots is the increasing racial consciousness of the Negro community and its concomitant drive to gain control of what is perceived to be theirs—the Negro community. While to a great extent this has always been the case with ethnic minorities, it assumes even greater importance for the Negro subgroup. This is a result of the fact that, given the nature of our society and his skin color, the Negro is inevitably identified with his group—he cannot, like previous groups, easily escape it—and that the issue of autonomy is of central importance to the Negro. Control of his neighborhood is almost synonymous with self-respect and the attainment of manhood. But neighborhood control is difficult to achieve. The skills necessary must be taught and Negroes have been denied access to the institutions that teach them. In addition, white institutions, legal and criminal, were already present in the cities to which the Negro migrated and he thus found himself under the control of forces who use him in his own neighborhood. In the face of such powerful forces, there are some people who feel that there remains but one way to evict outsiders and that is through civil disturbance. Though they are small in number (though perhaps larger in influence), at least some of the more ideological groups may have become involved in the riot for this reason.[18]

The fifth background cause of the riots and one that has been implied above is that there has been an increase in the level of expectation with insufficient actual improvement.[19] This increases the tension level and opens the door for feelings of frustration. It is, after all, not usually the defeated and downtrodden who revolt. Usually, such people avoid active involvement and become apathetic, or retreat into uncomplicated religions that promise them both the compensation of an afterlife and the assurance that the rich will suffer in the afterlife. It is rather those with hope, who have at one time or another taken the American equalitarian dream seriously or those who can now see the possibility of living a better life who become activists. This is why poverty and discrimination alone are not sufficient explanations of riot or revolt and why eliminating only poverty, however important that

18. P. Lowinger, C. Darrow, and F. Huige, "Case Study of the Detroit Uprising," *Archives of General Psychiatry,* 21 (1969):33-38.
19. Part of the change in expectation is a shift in reference group selection. As Pettigrew, op. cit., p. 187, puts it, "Slowly, imperceptibly, the frame of reference for many Negro Americans has shifted during the past few decades. While formerly most Negroes judged how well off they were by their own previous conditions, the rising expectations of the present are increasingly framed in terms of the wider society. Negro protest today is moving away from an exclusive emphasis upon desegregation and equal opportunity toward a broader demand for a 'fair share' and advantages directly comparable to those of whites. This shift merits special attention, for the actual gains just reviewed were all relative to previous Negro conditions. But such advances are not enough to meet the hopes of a people beginning to contrast their still-lowly position with the rich abundance surrounding them. The hard truth is that the Negro's recent progress does not begin to close the gap between the two races."

is, cannot eliminate the root causes of revolt. It is probably true that the working class[20] rather than the middle class will become the activists because the middle class has been trained in greater social control and has more to lose than the working class. But even middle-class individuals empathize with the more aggressive ones and may provide covert support and sometimes that most critical element—leadership.

New hope is created in part by real but partial gains, by promises, and by changes in outlook. The example of black Africans achieving independence, Supreme Court decisions, civil rights legislation, the civil rights movement, the hopes of the Great Society, and the removal of some barriers have been key influences in the creation of hope. It is clear that in the past few years, however, we have made many promises and that we have not kept most of them. This is not only because national attention and resources are focused on Vietnam but also because to carry out the promises, made or implied, more trained personnel to do the job and far greater involvement by community leaders are needed. Perhaps even more important is the lack of fundamental changes in the attitudes and comprehension of whites. We have not faced up to the problem of integration in our society nor have we been willing to take the steps in the way of education, training, and remotivation that will help persons who currently lack necessary skills or do not strive as a logical and inevitable consequence of past practices. Until we do, we will always be in the position of not being able to keep many of the promises.

It should be clear that such a failure is dangerous. Our society had done well to provide such hope. No society can, practically or morally, permit a large group of people to reside in apathy and defeat cut off from the larger society. But providing hope and increased expectation creates an imperative to make good on the commitment. It cannot be stressed enough that when an oppressed people see freedom, the abuses they continue to live with become intolerable.*

To this point, discussion has centered about some of the underlying determinants of riots. Not dealt with to this point is what has been identified by some as a major determinant of riots—that is the nature of the riot process itself. To many persons a riot is little more than the release of man's

---

*Editor's Note: As indicated in the preface, the research literature provides evidence that relative deprivation and increasing expectations of change in social position occur in the urban context independent of white or black leadership promises or lack of promises.

20. The working class should not be confused with what has been called the "underclass." The working class are those individuals who have made some progress and have some hope but whose jobs are basically manual in nature (though not necessarily low-paying). The underclass are the defeated, often unemployed and unemployable, on welfare and the like. According to the relative deprivation hypothesis or social comparison theory described in this section, it should be the former, not the latter, group that takes action. As will be shown, this is exactly the case.

"baser instincts," instincts which are usually held in check by "civilized" moral codes. Riots are seen as events dominated by raw emotion and by the emergence of a "collective mind" within the crowd. As it progresses, this view asserts, the riot increasingly feeds on itself. Implied in this view is a theory of human behavior stressing the aggressive "instinct" and the transformation of behavior produced by the mob. In admittedly much simplified form, this is the basic theory put forth by the 19th century sociologist, LeBon, and one which has for years dominated thinking about riots.[21]

There is some truth to this view. Riots possess a highly emotional nature and it is clear that usual norms and previously operative ethical principles are often overridden. Further, the overthrow of these norms is facilitated by the releasing effects of large numbers of people violating them. Reports from Detroit, for instance (Kerner Report), talked of a "carnival" atmosphere during the early stages of the riot. Reliance on this view, however, is in major part misleading and what is not true about this formulation is very important.

First, the idea of a collective mind operating in unison is clearly contradicted by the fact that mobs show clear role differentiation. Some loot, some burn, some just watch, some inspire, some harangue, some pass rumors. The idea of a mindless crowd is contradicted by evidence that a large number of potential leaders strive to direct the crowds to their programs of action and that the crowd chooses between competing leadership. In this competition, it is people who have status as leaders of groups *before* the riot who have the advantage. It is very critical to note that the grievances existing before the riot began will often determine which activities and leaders are followed. As Hundley puts it:

Previous grievances that have been talked about in the community for some period of time represent pre-dispositions to act on the part of the crowd. The verbalized conclusions of the community rumor process, and the heightening of hostility prior to the riot, determine the magnitude and kind of activities.[22]

Second, the crowd when it chooses a course of action is not, as LeBon believed, a formless instinctually driven mob. Rather, it has adjusted its actions to the behavior of social control agencies such as the police. If the police are present but ineffective, intensified looting may occur. If the police are brutal, retaliation may occur.

Third, new norms and expectations as to what is right and wrong form and the crowd sets up its own notions of right and wrong.[23] These norms are

21. G. LeBon, *The Crowd* (1st ed., 1895) (New York: McGraw-Hill, 1951).
22. J. R. Hundley, Jr., "The Dynamics of Recent Ghetto Riots," *Journal of Urban Law,* 45 (1968):627-640.
23. R. Dynes and E. L. Quarantelli, "What Looting in Civil Disturbances Really Means," *Transaction,* 5 (1968):9-15. As Dynes and Quarantelli have pointed out, the phenomenon of looting in riots has as one of its determinants a redefinition of norms surrounding the nature of property and who is legitimately entitled to it. Looting, in their view, has something of the nature of a political act.

often different from those preceding the riot but they are norms nonetheless, however temporary they may be. For example, the norm may be that white businessmen exploit the Negro and should be burned out.

One of the important roles in the crowd is that of the instigator and exploiter. There is considerable evidence that loosely organized groups contributed to the setting of the mood that led to the outbreak and to its prolongation and intensification as well. It is likely these groups carried out much of the physical destruction. It should be explicitly stated that this does not mean that the riot was started or received its motive force through such groups nor that the riot would necessarily have run a different course without them. The weight of evidence as reported by the Kerner Commission supports the view that the riot was a predominantly spontaneous, unplanned, and expressive event throughout its course. However, such groups could easily operate within the broad confusion of the riot.

How much community support these groups have and how much they need to carry out their work is not known. Some people believe that such groups cannot operate without at least passive community support. Others feel that they can operate and cause great damage entirely without community support. What is clear about them, however, is that they are people whose minds are dangerously close to being closed. They feel that there is little that will be done to improve conditions, that these conditions are intolerable and they are increasingly prepared to go down fighting. It is doubtful that in their highly suspicious and angry state they can be reasoned with. Perhaps there is in reality little that can be said to them since promises have been made and not kept. Changing them is not the critical issue in any case. Currently a very small minority, the ultimate danger they present may be that they will draw people who are angry and frustrated to their side, increasing polarization and inviting white hostile counter-reaction. The short-run damage they can cause may be of lesser ultimate importance.

What has been presented to this point is a social scientist's analysis of some of the causes of urban riots with racial overtones and a discussion of riots themselves. The review has been analytical and fairly general. To fully understand rioting behavior, it is important to find out what the lay person feels, for, after all, he is the one who determines social behavior. Also needed is a close look at the public, rioters and non-rioters alike, to find out in far greater detail about how the social institutions to which they belong, their education, their job status, and so on, affect their behavior. Critical too are citizens' hopes and fears for the future, both their personal futures and the future of race relations in the United States. The summer of 1967 was the fourth summer of major urban riots and by far the worst, and the cumulative effect of this rioting on whites and Negroes alike is a matter of considerable importance. Some specific questions are these: What kinds of persons played a role in the riots? How do rioters and non-rioters, white and Negro, explain the riot—do they see it along social protest lines or as an expression of base human motives? What do their views portend for the future? What do the people charged with keeping public order, the police, feel about these events? Is the white community more or less responsive to the needs of the Negro as a result of civil disturbance? Do Negroes feel that rioting behavior is a valid form of social action?

Our study was designed to answer these and other questions. Below are described the groups interviewed and what was asked of them.

Design of the Study

The reaction to the riot of individuals in four discernible groups was investigated using exploratory projective interviewing techniques. The groupings were (1) persons arrested in the riot, the closest the study came to an "action" group; (2) non-riot participants in the black community within the cities of Detroit, Highland Park, and Hamtramck; (3) members of the white community within the cities of Detroit, Highland Park, and Hamtramck; and (4) Detroit police officers.

All the aforementioned groups were questioned about their attitudes toward the riot and their explanations of its causes. There were also questions about the general character of race relations and the opportunity structure in Detroit. In the community sample only, there were a number of questions relating to political attitudes, and in the police sample there were numerous questions related to police work and police reaction to the riot events. Finally, in all the samples, respondents were queried about their family structure, employment history, educational history, other demographic characteristics, and satisfaction with their lives.

The interviewers were mostly experienced survey interviewers but smaller numbers of high school teachers and psychology students, trained by our staff, were employed. The race of the interviewers was matched to the race of the respondents with the exception of the police survey where, for several reasons, it was decided to use white interviewers for both black and white officers.*

Findings

The findings to be reported herein are the central ones of the study. The findings are not necessarily presented in the order of their importance.

*EDITOR'S NOTE: The projective techniques employed in this investigation were influenced by the timing factor. The study occurred within weeks of the riot in 1967. The aim was to secure data in context of the high emotional atmosphere generated immediately after the riot. This approach is in contrast to Warren's careful random selection process a year later reporting quantitative as well as qualitative data. See: Donald Warren "Community Dissensus" in part three.

First, regardless of the specific group studied, there is a major difference in interpretation between the races. The predominant view within the white community is that the riot was the result of agitators, the desire of people to take things, the temper of the times, or the pursuit of what might be called "undisciplined self-interest." A large minority of whites, however, think that the riot was due to mistreatment of Negroes or the economic or social disadvantages Negroes live under.[24] Two-thirds of whites believe the riot was planned in advance. The overwhelming majority of whites see the riot as leading to negative results and reported a loss of sympathy for problems of the Negro American. Negroes, however, overwhelmingly see the riot as due to mistreatment or the economic or social disadvantages Negroes live under, rarely blame agitators or the temper of the times, and are less likely to attribute the riot to the pursuit of "undisciplined self-interest" or the desire to take things. Again, in contrast with whites, the overwhelming majority of Negroes see the riot as *not* planned in advance. Negroes split into three approximately equal groups with regard to outcome—those seeing gain, those seeing loss, and those seeing no change. Negroes are evenly split into expectations of increased white sympathy and expectations of decreased white sympathy.[25]

Despite this interpretation by Negroes, some sympathy for the rioters among about half the black group, and an increase rather than a decrease in pride in being Negro, there is profound conflict and a great deal of mixed feelings about the riot. Only a small minority have anything positive to say about the events of the riot (e.g., burning, looting, violence, etc.). It is almost as if many were saying, "Some kind of protest was necessary but the form was wrong." Clearly the riot frightened both black and white citizens and the closer to the riot the more frightened were the individuals.

While agreement between the races on riot etiology is not frequent, they did agree that the riot was *not* caused by hoodlums, riffraff, or communists

24. Those whites with at least some college experience are more likely to see the riot as a protest—indeed with this group it is the most popular explanation. Among the Negro group, however, there is relatively little interpretive difference as a function of class or whether arrested or not.

25. The difference in interpretation by race applies to police officers as well. Though there are important differences between the police and community in numerous areas, there is a remarkable correspondence over the main themes of why the riot occurred and its likely outcome. Below the executive and upper command levels, white officers, most of whom are from working class backgrounds, strongly agree with the working class white community in not ascribing the riot to protest motives though they are much more likely than the white community to feel that lack of respect for law and order was a prime cause. Like the white community they see the riot as leading to negative results. (At the executive and upper command levels, however, the modal view, almost a majority in fact, was that the riot was a protest and was unplanned. In general, these officers have a more positive view of the black community than do lower echelon officers.) Black officers, like the black community, see protest as the prime cause and are split into the same three groups as to likely outcome. Unlike their white colleagues, black officers do not attribute the riot to a lack of respect for law and order or the influence of agitators.

and that the riot was *not* black against white. Many whites, however, may not have singled out hoodlums as a riot cause because they characterize all or most black citizens that way.[26]

Second, the overwhelming majority of the Negro community continues to believe in integration rather than separation. Clearly, Negroes remain committed to the society.[27] This means equal opportunity in jobs, housing, and schools rather than necessarily side-by-side living. The black community is not revolutionary in the sense of seeking to overthrow; but it is revolutionary in its drive to confront the society and modify its practices. Put simply, Negroes "want in." The Negro community has considerable optimism that this will come to pass and in fact has considerable optimism in general.[28]

Third, Negroes arrested in the riot mostly come from a working class population (not the "underclass"). Since arrestees are one of the riot's activist groups, this is an important fact.[29] Further, the overwhelming majority of this group is without previous criminal records, is predominantly young, male, employed (mostly at good wages), and unmarried (though if not married usually living with one or more family members). They tend not to belong to groups of any kind and do not espouse an ideologically militant philosophy (except for a small minority). In fact, all but a few of the arrestees are without significant organizational or political involvement.[30]

26. The results presented above are remarkably similar to those found in other cities, see, *e.g.,* the Kerner Report, R. T. Morris and V. Jeffries, "The White Reaction Study," unpublished paper, Los Angeles Riot Study, 1967. However, though it is difficult to compare data over time when they are from different cities, it appears, when one compares Los Angeles and Detroit, that white sympathy has declined as riots have continued over time.

27. Two years later, according to a *Newsweek* poll (June 30, 1969), this remains the overwhelming sentiment. As Aberbach and Walker, using the Detroit data, show (J. Aberbach and J. Walker, "Black Power: White and Black Interpretations of a Political Slogan in the Riot Aftermath," paper presented at the meeting of the American Political Science Association, Boston, September, 1968), even the predominant interpretation of "black power" by Negroes has this connotation. Unfortunately, whites react to the slogan "black power" with fear and hostility. It should be added, however, that there is some evidence that the number advocating separation may be increasing, if for no other reason than the young are more likely to endorse it than the old. See, and compare, the support for separation reported by Hedegard (J. M. Hedegard, "Detroit Community Attitudes on Race and Urban Rioting," unpublished paper, Detroit Riot Study, 1969) (using 1967 data) and the June 30, 1969, *Newsweek* survey.

28. The optimism expressed is consistent with the hypothesis of rising hope and expectation, one of the postulated riot etiology factors.

29. There is no sure way of knowing who rioted. Arrestees may come the closest, at least in the sense they were on the streets. Still it should be recognized that many arrestees were not involved in criminal offenses and, conversely, many persons who were rioters were not arrested.

30. There is an at least partial similarity between the arrestees and the Paris crowd of the French Revolution who were craftsmen, shop-owners and laborers (G. Rudé, *The Crowd in the French Revolution* [New York: Oxford University Press, 1959]). This too is consistent with the idea that protest movements in part are acts of groups elevated out of apathy but not far enough "in" the society to have a full commitment to things as they currently are.

The arrestee unemployment rate is roughly equal to the black community as a whole (when controlled for age) and in interpretation of the riot and complaints about the social institutions of their community are not differentiable from the Negro community as a whole (except in their extreme hostility to the police, undoubtedly in major part a function of their age and arrest experience). Finally, like most Negro Detroiters, they are not recent arrivals. Most had either been born in Detroit or had migrated to the city at least ten years before the riot. Further most had come from Southern *cities* anyway. These findings are remarkably similar to those of Los Angeles.[31] "Urban shock" just does not explain riots.

Fourth, many whites have little comprehension of the plight of the Negro, the discrimination and impediments he must live with, and know little of Negro history. Not only have they not yet become convinced of the urgency of Negroes' drive for freedom, but many believe that Negroes are pushing too hard and already getting too much. For example, the overwhelming majority of white police officers feel that societal arrangements are the same for white and black or actually favor Negroes.[32] While, unfortunately, this question was not asked in the community survey, evidence from other surveys (see, e.g., *Newsweek*, October 6, 1969, Pettigrew) indicates this is a majority view among whites. Generally, it is clear that white attitudes and beliefs have moderated considerably in the post-war era but there remains a long way to go and there is the ever-present threat of a regression. It is fair to assert that whites continue to have considerably more direct, overt hostility toward Negroes than Negroes do for whites.

Fifth, in the Negro population, the younger the age, the more militant the respondent. For example, in the community group, the younger the person the more the anger at the police (the arrestee group's hostility to the police is so general that age plays no role).[33] The younger the age the more the liking for militant leaders and the more positive the feelings toward the riot and/or its anticipated consequences (though even in the youngest age group reaction to the events of the riot is predominantly negative).

This generalization may not apply to those under 18. They do not seem to have well-formed convictions about the riot, leadership or race relations. Rather they seem to lack information about the current situation, to know

31. R. J. Murphy and J. M. Watson, "The Structure of Discontent: The Relationship Between Social Structure, Grievance, and Support for the Los Angeles Riot," unpublished paper, Los Angeles Riot Study, 1967.
32. The potential for failure of communication and conflict because of these beliefs is high. Negroes, not unexpectedly, see themselves as discriminated against in all areas with jobs being the chief source of complaint.
33. The arrest experience in fact may well have created a group of strongly anti-police young men. Well over a majority of Negro arrestees reported police brutality of either a physical or verbal kind.

less in general about things, and perhaps not surprisingly to seem somewhat superficial and immature. This may have changed in the two years since the riot. The strongest convictions are found in those in their twenties. Many of them are very angry. Their anger is under better control but is more sharply focused.

Conclusions

The analysis of urban disturbances and the empirical data collected by our group and other researchers are reasonably harmonious and clearly point to a continuing and deepening social crisis whose outcome is much in doubt. On the one hand is a people impatient with the slow pace of change, increasingly determined to change their situation and ready to fight by any means a return to their previous status. Further, though there is argument over means, the drive has support throughout almost all segments of the Negro community. Riots, while not a desired consequence of this drive, show the truth of this basic fact. On the other hand is a white majority which controls all the important institutions and which, despite fifteen years of civil rights activity and five years of urban rioting, still does not sense the urgency of the Negro revolution, for it is precisely that. To be sure, there is, despite assertions that Negroes are treated fairly, at least a vague comprehension that the Negro has been grievously wronged; but there is, for most, neither the identification with the Negro cause nor the deep disturbance that generates action. Rather, there is a feeling of threat both in an immediate physical sense and in the sense of concern about loss of status, jobs, and the vested interests that groups in power tend to think are morally theirs. To date, the chief white reaction has been, aside from some programs of genuine value, flight, both psychological and physical, along with a potentially dangerous temptation to increasingly rely on the police to act as a buffer between them and the Negro population. Summing up, the Negro is prone to see the lack of progress as a cause of the riots while whites see "giving" the Negro some of his long-deferred rights as the cause of the riots. These differing responses occur in the context of increasing violence, fear, and the rising expectancies that drive the black community.

It would be a great loss if the outcome of the black drive for equality were to fail. This is so not only because of the threat of interracial violence and likely repression as a consequence of such violence but because the nation would have missed an unparalleled opportunity to reform those aspects of American society in need of change. If the nation is to succeed, we would be wise to heed the words of Kenneth Clark:

Continuing evidence of the persuasive moral apathy and political cynicism in the American mass culture is a significant negative in weighing the possibilities of social democracy. If constructive change were to depend on the chance of profound moral conversion, there might be cause for pessimism. *Negroes must convince the majority, who are white, that continued oppression of the Negro minority hurts the white majority too.* Nor is it sophistry to argue that this is indeed the case. If it were not the case, the Negro cause would be helpless. Certainly the Negro cannot hope to argue his case primarily in terms of ethical concerns, for these historically have had only sentimental and verbal significance in themselves. They have never been the chief source of power for that social change which involves significant alteration of status between privileged versus unprivileged groups. Child labor legislation was not the direct result of moral indignation against the exploitation of children in factories, mines, mills, but rather reflected a growing manpower shortage and the new rise of the labor unions. *The value of ethical appeals is to be found only when they can be harnessed to more concrete appeals such as economic, political, or other power advantages to be derived from those with the power to facilitate or inhibit change.* Ethical and moral appeal can be used to give theoretical support for *a program of action,* or in some cases to obscure and make the pragmatic aspects of that program more palatable to conscience. If moral force opposes economic or political ends, the goal of moral force may be postponed. The reverse may also be true. But where moral force and practical advantage are united, their momentum is hard to deny [emphasis added].[34]

34. K. B. Clark, *Dark Ghetto: Dilemmas of Social Power* (New York: Harper & Row Publishers, 1965), p. 204.

Emergent Communal Response

Thomas R. Forrest

Introduction

. . . it just so happened that on Sunday morning I had said in the pulpit that I had just finished a tour of the ghetto in Detroit and that if anyone thought that Detroit was going to escape violence we were badly mistaken. I think my complete statement was that if we were able to escape it this summer we would have it by next summer. At that point the riots were already in progress but no one knew it. That evening my wife and I were looking at the TV coverage of the Israeli-Arab conflict and they interrupted the program to say that the Grand Rapids National Guard would report to their center. We heard that announcement a couple of times and I said to my wife that it looked like there was trouble in Grand Rapids. If there was I would probably head for Grand Rapids. I called our Association Minister and asked him what was happening in Grand Rapids and he said he didn't know what was happening at Grand Rapids—all he knew was what was happening in Detroit. And I said, "well, what do you mean?" And he said, "well, the whole innercity looks like it's about to break open." So that was Sunday night.

The above quote from a minister, who would later become involved in the Interfaith Emergency Center, summarizes several facts concerning events in Detroit, Michigan, on Sunday, July 23, 1967. First, certain persons in the Detroit community were sensitive to possible trouble that might erupt into a full-scale disturbance. Second, most of Detroit's citizens were totally unaware of events occurring in their city. City and state officials received the news media's cooperation in down-playing the event, so that local officials would obtain some control over the situation. However, national affiliates in other cities were reporting the events happening in Detroit. And third, most citizens learned of the disturbance through many indirect channels.

Work on this article was supported in part by the Center for Studies of Mental Health and Social Problems, Applied Research Branch, U.S. Public Health Service National Institute of Mental Health Grant 5-R01-MH15399-02. The author is on the staff of the Ohio State University Disaster Research Center. This article is previously unpublished.

July 23, for most individuals, was a normal summer Sunday, with regular church attendance, swim meets, backyard barbecues, and a Tiger's home baseball game. Unknown to the 34,000 persons attending the Tiger's game, ten blocks from Tiger Stadium a disturbance was well underway. While many had taken their transistor radios to the game, no reports by local stations were given concerning any city disorder. The first clues that many received occurred when leaving the stadium. They found numerous roadblocks closing off the affected area. Belle Isle, a small recreational area, located in the Detroit River, was to have a swim meet Sunday afternoon. Those who were to attend found that the entire island had been closed. For many who had experienced the 1943 riot, this occurrence recalled the closing of Belle Isle—and its use as a place of internment. Slowly, other clues of a city-wide disturbance were reaching the people.

For the greater part of Sunday, Detroit was under a news blackout. Local newspapers had already gone to press and the radio and TV stations cooperated in keeping silence on the disturbance taking place in the Twelfth Street area. It was felt by city officials that by down-playing the incident police officials could somehow contain it and minimize the spread of violence. But rumors spread rapidly and by the late afternoon the telltale signs of black smoke, oozing forth into the sky, finally alerted everyone that something unusual was happening in Detroit. By Sunday evening, July 23, few people doubted that Detroit was in for trouble, but the extent and intensity of the disturbance was not yet comprehended. Despite the local news blackout, several clergymen and other isolated individuals had received disturbance reports from friends, relatives, and denominational headquarter officials, located in other metropolitan cities. While local Detroit radio and TV stations were down-playing the whole disturbance, national radio and TV affiliates were reporting the complete sequence of events. Individuals in other cities called friends and relatives in Detroit, only to find that they knew nothing of the disturbance. By 4:20 P.M. Detroit's Mayor requested that the National Guard be brought into the city, with the first troops arriving by 7:00 P.M. By 7:45 P.M. the Mayor issued a proclamation instituting a 9:00 P.M. to 5:00 A.M. curfew.

With the curfew and news blackout preventing both travel into the area and the dispensing of authenticated information, interested citizens relied upon gossip and what other bits and pieces of information they could gather from friends. That evening numerous Detroit church officials began calling their churches in the affected area to ascertain the extent of the disturbance, to inquire about the threat to church property and also to insure local pastors that the denomination would do all it could to aid them in their efforts to meet the situation. Reports were relayed back to these officials as to the widespread looting and arson taking place before the clergymen's eyes; however, no church reported that its property was in any way jeopardized, burned or looted. Ministers and priests were encouraged to walk the streets in their clerical garb in order to try and persuade individuals to refrain from looting and burning. The widespread destruction testified to the ineffectiveness of this effort.

Emergent Process

In most crisis situations, individuals seek to understand and interpret events by turning to friends and acquaintances for reassurance. The role that these previous relationships play should be underscored, for these relationships often provide the basis for much of the coordinated response to a crisis.

The onset of Detroit's civil disturbance was not the first time that clergymen and religious lay leaders had come together to handle existing community social needs such as low-cost housing, neighborhood integration, job discrimination, and the myriad of other problems associated with poverty and racial discrimination. Besides the normal contacts through interfaith committees, councils and special study groups, church officials (primarily those church executives freed from pastoral duties) have been in frequent contact with one another concerning Detroit's racial and poverty problems. During 1963 and 1964 interested church officials formed the Metropolitan Religion and Race Conference (later Council for Race and Human Rights), which was involved in many of the nonviolent protests that characterized the earlier era of the civil rights movement. However, since 1965 with the civil rights position dramatically changing towards a more militant orientation, many of the basic nonviolent premises which the council supported were being usurped by the more militant civil rights groups. This undermined the effectiveness of the conference to speak and be heard. As one member stated:

We had an interfaith organization, The Metropolitan Council for Race and Religion and Human Rights back in the civil rights movement in 1963 and 1964—four faith groups and we did a pretty good job. Then with that nonviolent phase of the civil rights movement ended we sort of lost our reason for existence it seemed. The organization spun off into kind of beating the bushes and going through motions. We still maintain it in name and we occasionally issue a statement from time to time on some public issue.

On returning from Chicago in January, 1967, a United Church of Christ official brought back to Detroit an idea that he had acquired in Chicago concerning an interfaith "hotline." This "hotline" was a telephone conference among church officials involved in missions work. (Missions work is essentially the social-action field of the denominational structure.) The phone conference in Chicago was primarily intended as an opportunity to discuss the race-relation problems existing in the metropolitan area without having to spend time travelling to and from a meeting place. Financially, those involved felt that it would be cheaper to have a phone conference. It was then suggested to the Metropolitan Detroit Council of Churches that this type of conference would be an advantageous undertaking on the part of Detroit church officials interested in social programs. At the end of January, 1967, an executive of the Detroit Council of Churches arranged a phone conference to be conducted at 8:00 A.M., Monday mornings. These Monday morning conferences were soon to be labeled the "Monday morning hotline," patterned after the Chicago one. Ten members comprised the core of this group, representing the Metropolitan Detroit Council of Churches, Methodist, Episcopal, Presbyterian and United Church of Christ headquarters, along with the Catholic Archdiocese of Detroit and the Protestant Community Services.

Every Monday morning at 8:00 A.M. the conference is held with a loose agenda allowing each member to contribute what he feels is important. Discussions run from how the churches could aid Negro families who move into an all-white neighborhood, to the Kodak conflict with the Congress of Racial Equality (CORE) in Rochester, New York.[1] A substantial portion of each meeting was centered around informing one another as to problems (mainly poverty and racial matters) posed in the Detroit metropolitan community. The confidence and informal understandings that participants gained through these conference calls would play a crucial role in the initial emergence of the Interfaith Council and Center.* As one member stated:

. . . the fact that we all knew each other well enough so that when we sat together Monday afternoon we didn't have to say now who is this guy, can I trust him? I mean there had been a band of confidence built up that we immediately could move together.

---

*At this point it would be appropriate to distinguish between the Interfaith Emergency Center and Council. Both the center and council emerged from this meeting. The council was designated to act as the governing body for all interfaith activities, while the center became the operating arm of the council during the emergency period (July 24-August 4). Throughout this period the council held daily meetings to assess the events and to determine the future course of action to be taken by the collective interfaith body. With the establishment of the council, four committees were formed to carry out its activities. One committee was responsible for the center; another assessed what community needs could be fulfilled by the council; third, a finance committee was formed to handle all monetary donations to the council; and last, a long-range planning committee was formed to plan future council responses. While the council and center had the same basic roots, they both had distinct and separate histories which for the purpose of this article will be confined to the Interfaith Emergency Center. While the council was technically the governing body of the center, in actuality the center was an autonomous unit, developing its own separate structure, leadership, and areas of involvement.

1. The Eastman Kodak conflict with CORE in the spring of 1967 centered around alleged accusations by CORE that the Eastman Kodak Company practiced racial discrimination in the hiring of employees. Members of the hotline discussed how the clergy could bring pressure to bear upon Kodak.

While the Monday morning hotline provided one basis for interaction, the other groups (Detroit Council of Churches, Metropolitan Council on Religion and Human Rights, and many other committees and conferences) all helped to establish a firm foundation of friendship and trust. With these past associations it logically followed that these individuals would attempt to contact one another when civic disorder gripped Detroit.

Several ministers had made a special point to be in their offices early Monday morning in hopes of receiving the hotline conference call, but no call came through. Information was still scarce, with the news media just starting to give details of the disturbance. An Episcopalian executive, in an effort to assess what had happened, heard of a meeting of the Interdenominational Ministerial Alliance (a Negro minister's association) and decided to attend this meeting since he was unable to contact members of the hotline. This meeting lasted three hours with no course of action decided upon. It was decided to reconvene the meeting the following day. Meanwhile, throughout the morning members of the hotline had contacted one another. It was decided by a Methodist official to convene a general meeting of the hotline members, plus other interested members of the religious community. A special effort was made to invite members of the Jewish Community Council and Interdenominational Ministerial Alliance. Anxious to hear the report of two clergymen, who, as members of the City Coordinating Commission, met earlier that afternoon with the mayor, they decided to hold the general meeting at 3:00 P.M. Simultaneously, an executive of the Detroit Council of Churches was also calling denominational officials for a 3:00 P.M. meeting. Since many of the individuals called were asked to attend both meetings, it was decided to combine the two meetings. Thus, the meeting originally intended for the 10 hotline members actually turned out to be attended by 20-25 individuals.

Although not all of the individuals who attended the 3:00 P.M. meeting had made previous contact with one another, a central core of "hotline" participants had. As stated by one member, a certain confidence existed between members which enabled them to respond. Many of the members had common predispositions in that each had been involved in social action programs. What exactly was the motivation of each individual is difficult to assess. It may have been humanitarian desires, idealism, guilt, religious obligation, frustration, the coincidence of a scheduled hotline conference, or a combination of these and many other factors. However, what is important in understanding the emergent process is that having had previous contact with one another these individuals sought out each other to find some meaning to the crisis and to arrive at a course of action.

The 3:00 P.M. meeting was held in the third floor office of the Director of Human Relations, Division of the Community Affairs Department of the

Archdiocese of Detroit, located in the Gabriel Richard Building. Members of the City Coordinating Commission reported that the city was not doing much outside of providing primary police and fire protection. The first hour was spent exchanging information that each had gathered by either being out in the streets and/or talking with participants or agents of control (police or fire officials).

In exchanging what little information that had been gathered, the group as a whole was searching for meaning in order to understand the crisis. Meaning was found through verbal communication concerning what happened and through sifting and sorting the explanations offered. At the meeting individuals looked to others to help structure the situation. By verbalizing observations and questioning what and why events occurred, the crisis situation was structured so that individuals could understand and relate to what had happened.

Having had previous experience in the Watts disturbance, the Episcopal Society for Culture and Racial Unity (ESCRU), an unofficial organization of the Episcopal Church, drew up a set of plans which detailed suggestions as to the role the church could play in a civil disturbance. The plan called for an interfaith response which would refrain from offering gratuitous calls for law and order, while trying to see what creative things could be done. One suggestion in the ESCRU plan was the establishment of an information center which would collect and dispense information related to the disturbance. With this plan in mind, an Episcopal official present at the meeting suggested that for the moment any immediate interpretation of the events should be postponed. Instead, this group should refrain from making statements calling for law and order and strive to establish a constructive course of action.

While the collective body did not reach consensus on interpreting the crisis, a decision was reached with respect to the immediate circumstance facing those present. It was decided to follow the ESCRU suggestion and refrain from a call for law and order. The expressed intent of this group was that they remain neutral in whatever role they were to perform. Once this had been decided the next step was to commit those present to a given course of action.

Again referring to the ESCRU plan, the Episcopal official made the motion that an information center be formed. A vote was taken and the motion accepted unanimously. Immediately following the vote, the same official volunteered the use of the Episcopal Diocesan Center. It was suggested that this building would be appropriate because it was near the disturbance area but yet not in it. It also had a large parking lot, numerous phones, and ample office space. Having committed themselves to a given course of action and accepted the physical facilities with which to operate, those present established the Interfaith Emergency Center.

It is at this point that events became entangled with respect to the overall activities of IEC. For clarity, we will first present a general overview followed by a more detailed discussion focusing upon the areas of community acceptance, operating structure, volunteer assistance, and general responses.

General Overview

From those present at the 3:00 P.M. meeting, seven volunteered to man the newly formed Interfaith Information Center. Shortly after the 6:00 P.M. newscast, which announced the existence of IEC, calls started coming into the center. While it was anticipated that a majority of calls would be concerned with information requests, it was not anticipated that these calls would come from individuals asking how they could volunteer their help or how they could obtain help. It became evident that the basic need was for a brokerage which would connect individual needs with community resources and services. For the remainder of Monday evening and well into the early morning hours of Tuesday, July 25, aid was handled on an individual basis.

Early Tuesday morning it became apparent (from calls received from suburban churches volunteering to collect food and clothing, and from calls received from urban churches volunteering their services as centers for distributing food and clothing) that a network was needed to link resources located in the suburbs with needs existing in affected areas. Individuals working at the center believed that if they could respond by connecting needs with appropriate resources, the dual problematic situation of supply and demand could be solved. Fortunately at this time the Wayne County AFL-CIO (UAW) Council had heard of the center's existence and volunteered to act as a transportation service. Using volunteer truck drivers and trucks donated by major companies in the greater metropolitan area, the union established a distribution department dispatching drivers to 25 collection centers and 21 distribution centers.

The remainder of the week saw a fairly adaptive structure develop which was able to adjust to incoming demands. By Saturday, July 29, a plan had been developed to systematically phase out the food operation. A news release, given at 11:00 A.M. Saturday, explained the gradual phase out of the 25 collection centers and 21 distribution centers over a four-day period. A list was provided naming each center and its closing date. From July 30 to August 4, IEC gradually phased out its coordination of the centers.

As it turned out, by Monday July 30, the dozen individuals still working at the center realized that a whole new set of problems faced individuals who had suffered from the disturbance. These new problems became the basis for the continuance of IEC. It was to continue in operation for almost an additional four months.

Community Acceptance

Once the Interfaith Emergency Center (IEC) had emerged, the first problem it faced was to make the center known to the general public. It was decided around 5:00 P.M., Monday, that a news release should be prepared for the 6:00 P.M. radio and television newscast. The announcement stated that the IEC had come into existence to aid individual citizens requesting information. The mass media (radio and television), acted as a mediator, providing IEC with the necessary minimum legitimacy so that it would be recognized by individuals and other organizations within the community.

The initial IEC announcement was well received by the community. For a variety of reasons many of the welfare agencies and community emergency agencies (*i.e.*, Red Cross and Civil Defense) were not responding in an effective manner. On Monday, July 24, the public and many private welfare agencies closed in response to the city-wide curfew. It was not until Tuesday, July 24, or Wednesday, July 25, that welfare agencies opened to respond to the growing needs. Even though the normal welfare agencies had opened by Wednesday, many individuals had heard of IEC and preferred to come to IEC instead of the city agencies. One volunteer explained this behavior by stating:

. . . the public welfare, you know, would have been inundated with requests for help. But the head of public welfare told us that day at the mayor's office that although he had announced over the radio, and I think there had been announcements in the paper, that he had put I think something like twenty extra staff members on. The first day after those announcements he had—I've forgotten 4 or 40. Either one is ridiculous. Anyway just a tiny number of applications. And several people at the meeting pointed out that a great many of these people simply did not want to go to public welfare. . . . Welfare does an enormous job in the city, but it doesn't have the best reputation in the world for efficiency or for politeness and courtesy.

The fact that IEC was able to respond quickly without the red tape and stigma normally associated with welfare agencies may have been the reason why many individuals turned to IEC for aid. With individuals feeling that they could turn to IEC, other community groups were also seeking organization which would perform the social welfare function. While welfare agencies were closed on Monday, Red Cross and civil defense were not responding as normally anticipated. Red Cross's problem centered around the legality of its participation in a civil disturbance. Red Cross has a legal mandate which requires it to respond to natural disasters. However, its charter was ambiguous in its definition of its role in a civil disturbance.[2] In

2. At the annual convention of the American Red Cross in Denver, Colorado, May 6, 1968, a policy statement was adopted by the National Board of Governors. This statement made the local Red Cross chapter's role one of supplementing efforts of civil authorities in event of a civil disturbance.

an official policy statement from Red Cross headquarters, Red Cross Chapters were directed during a civil disturbance to maintain close contact with civic authorities, and ". . . if there is suffering and want from any cause and fundamental human needs are not being met, Red Cross Chapters may participate in community action in extending relief."[3] However, any participation would not be reimbursed by the national chapter; any expenditure of funds would have to be financed through a local campaign for funds. The lack of funds and the ambiguities in Red Cross's role led it to curtail its activities.

With the welfare agencies and two primary community emergency organizations either not operative or operating on a limited basis, the Interfaith action was viewed as a positive act by other community organizations. Individual citizens and organizations quickly acted to legitimatize IEC.

One of the first public offices to recognize IEC was the mayor's office. Through this office, official contacts were made with other community organizations. The mayor's formal recognition provided the necessary legitimacy to integrate IEC into the total community emergency response. By attending many city-wide coordinating meetings, interfaith personnel were able to establish working relationships with nearly all governmental offices, law enforcement agencies, social welfare centers, and the local AFL-CIO (UAW) council.

Shortly after its emergency, IEC obtained an agreement with the police and National Guard which permitted IEC volunteers to travel during curfew (9:00 P.M-5:00 A.M.). Large signs stating "Interfaith Emergency Food Distribution Center" were attached to delivery trucks. Apparently these signs were sufficient legitimate symbols since, as one individual stated, ". . . none of them (trucks and truck drivers) suffered any injury or scratch even going into an area where a riot was existing after dark—both sides sort of accepted them in the spirit of humanitarians coming in to relieve the community." Volunteers who found it necessary to travel to and from their homes were also issued passes honored by both the police and National Guard.

While nearly all organizations accepted the role the IEC played during the disturbance, a severe conflict arose between IEC and the local civil defense. About a month and a half before the disturbance, civil defense suffered a severe cutback in personnel and funds as a direct result of a city-budget cut. A provision had been made that, in emergencies, former civil defense personnel would return to their previous positions. (In reality only a fraction returned.) However, the occurrence of the disturbance provided the unique opportunity for civil defense to again re-assert its influence and to show the larger community that it indeed had a valuable part to play in community emergencies.

3. The American National Red Cross, "American Red Cross Responsibility in Situations Caused by Economic, Political and Social Emergencies, April 17, 1967" (Washington: The American National Red Cross, 1967). (Policy Statement.)

Late Sunday evening (July 23) and early Monday morning, civil defense established five temporary shelters in three large Catholic churches and two public schools. Each shelter was equipped to accommodate for sleeping 300 to 500 persons. However, on Tuesday at a coordinating meeting held in the civil defense office, IEC and civil defense confronted one another in a struggle to designate their respective task areas. Civil defense saw IEC's emergency role as illegitimate and infringing upon its own duties. On the other hand, IEC felt that since it had developed an effective collection and distribution network recognized by the mayor's office that civil defense could not force it to curtail its emergency activities. The conflict centered around the IEC operational procedures in the distribution center. Persons coming to distribution centers were not required to verify their needs, instead food was dispensed to whomever entered the center. This, civil defense felt, only prolonged the return to normal commercial activities and encouraged fradulent behavior. Although IEC realized that many persons were taking advantage of the distribution centers, they felt that rather than allowing individuals with legitimate needs to go hungry, they would overlook the few who took advantage. While no simple solution was arrived at, IEC did agree to phase out its distribution centers as soon as it could be assured that neighborhood stores were operating or that other community agencies would provide for the existing social needs.

Operating Structure

Monday evening, operations at the center were handled by seven individuals—four of whom came directly from the 3:00 P.M. meeting, while the other three heard indirectly from their own denominational officials that an interfaith effort was being undertaken. All seven volunteers were ministers representing the Episcopal, Lutheran, Methodist, and United Church of Christ churches. Opening the switchboard and finding someone to man it was the first problem faced by the group. The role of operator was assigned to one minister who had previous experience operating a switchboard, while the other volunteers just sat down and started to answer the phone. As one minister stated: "There was no chance for job description, no chance for job planning." That evening, realizing that more volunteers would be needed, an announcement was made over radio and television, requesting volunteers to staff the newly formed center.

Monday evening was primarily spent answering calls from frustrated and desperate individuals in the disturbance area, while also receiving calls from persons wishing to volunteer their help. The following volunteer's comment summarizes the first evening's activities:

. . . the kind of call we'd gotten during the night was, for example, a woman with a four-day-old baby in the riot area who had run out of formula for the child.

Or a diabetic who had run out of insulin—didn't have the proper food—or the blind were calling in and they were just plain frightened, completely disorientated, and they needed food supplies of one kind or another. So what we needed then was volunteer drivers—people who would go out and get the stuff for us and take it to the address. So I put out a call for volunteers and the response was overwhelming.

With this limited base of operation, the response the first evening was restricted to contacting local ministers in the disturbance area, relaying the calls from distressed individuals in requesting that the local minister try to handle the problem. In extreme emergencies, a police precinct station, located across the street from the center, was contacted to see if it could check out the call and deliver whatever aid was necessary. The police precinct station would play a significant role during the remainder of the disturbance, by supplying information concerning the extent and location of the disturbance while also handling emergency requests.

The remainder of the first night consisted of answering calls and trying to match appropriate resources with particular needs. It was anticipated that individuals would want information regarding situational reports; what actually occurred were requests for help plus donations of services and resources. The change in the anticipated demands required a reassessment of the center's purpose. Early Tuesday, July 25, it was realized that the need was not for an information center, but instead for a broker to connect needs with appropriate resources.

The first of several major structural developments occurred Tuesday morning, July 25. As persons began tuning their radios to the morning news programs, they heard an announcement which gave a telephone number to call for information and aid. Immediately following the 6:00 A.M. newscast the switchboard received many calls and within a few hours was jammed with calls. With the requests exceeding the capability to respond, one individual took the initiative to organize the apparent chaotic situation. Following is an account of the initial organization:

. . . it was chaos on Tuesday at the center and nothing, no organization as such, had been established except the barest kind of answering phones. We were working in several offices and all of those offices were taking all kinds of calls. So at that point on Tuesday when they said that I was being placed in charge of the center, I then went to the switchboard and asked the girl to close the switchboard down for five minutes. And she did. Then I assembled all the staff together in one of those offices and superimposed a system. I had no idea that it would last. In fact, it was just an effort to bring some sort of organization to what we were trying to do and at that time I said one office, and pointed it out, would be the office where the operator will direct all calls from people who have needs, any kind of needs. Then there would be a resource office where the operator will direct all of the calls of resources—where we can get the resources we need. And then there will be a volunteer's office of people who want to volunteer themselves and whatever. And then there will be an office to coordinate the distribution center. This latter office was to coordinate the attempts by the outlying centers to get stuff to the distribution centers and then coordinate which distribution center was closest to the person that had the need who called in.

By Wednesday afternoon a fairly stable structure was developed with key leadership positions identified and tasks allocated to particular departments. *Figure 1* illustrates this structure.

A brief description of each position and department will provide an overview of the responsibilities of each.

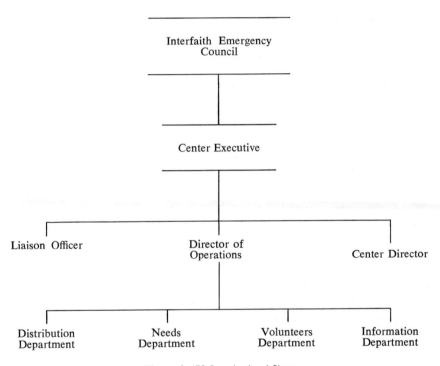

Figure 1. IEC Organizational Chart

The *center executive* was the individual responsible for the overall action of the IEC. It was his duty to report back to the council in the form of verbal progress reports specifying operational problem areas. At the center his duties were to oversee all activities, confirm and make decisions involving major operational changes, grant permission for use of financial donations, represent the center to the press and attend city-wide coordinating meetings and meetings with other community organizations.

The majority of interorganizational and community contacts were handled by a *liaison officer*. Much of this individual's time was spent representing IEC at co-ordinating sessions with the Mayor's Committee on Human Resource Development, civil defense, Red Cross, and other organizations who played a significant role in relation to the center.

Crucial to the whole operation of the center was the *center director* who was responsible for the initial structural breakdown and later operational refinements. It was his responsibility to see that the actual tasks were carried out, to make reassessments and adaptations, to the demands placed upon the center, to evaluate each department head, to arrange for needed materials and personnel, and to work closely with the center executive in the overall coordination of the center. Two individuals filled this position, one working a day shift and the other the night shift.

Similarly the *director of operations* also was a position held by two individuals working on a shift basis. Coordinating the appropriate resources with the specific need was the basic task of the director of operations. Information concerning the particular need for specific quantities of food was received through the needs and information department. These requests were then matched with the appropriate resource. This information was then passed on to the distribution department which was coordinated by the AFL-CIO (UAW).

The *distribution department* was operated by volunteer staff from the Wayne County AFL-CIO (UAW) Council. This department dispatched trucks to pick up food and clothing at designated collection centers and delivered these items to specific distribution centers.

A staff of social workers volunteered their services in operating a *needs department*. Incoming calls requesting aid from residents in affected areas were recorded by the social workers who have had extensive experience in handling these types of calls. If the need could not be met by the center, individuals were directed to the nearest distribution center. Otherwise, special arrangements were made to aid the individual by sending a volunteer to the individual or by referring the individual to an agency that could help.

With the influx of *volunteers* a special *department* had to be formed to coordinate the placement of volunteers into appropriate departments, arrange shifts, inform volunteers of changes with the center, introduce volunteers to appropriate department leaders and to generally oversee that each department was adequately staffed for each shift.

The *information department* was formed to handle calls requesting instructions as to the location of distribution and/or collection centers, name and location of appropriate agencies to contact for a particular problem, and location of areas affected by the disturbance.

Volunteer Assistance

On Monday evening, July 24, when it became apparent that more volunteers would be required to adequately staff the center, IEC announced over radio and television that it could use additional volunteers. By midmorning,

Tuesday, the response was so great that they had to turn volunteers away. Instead of calling into the center—which was extremely difficult to do—volunteers converged at the center, filling hallways and adding to the general confusion that already existed.* Since a general city-wide curfew had technically closed down the city, individuals were freed from their normal employment duties to be able to volunteer their time.

Among the volunteers that eventually participated in IEC, social workers played an important role. Persons calling to request individual aid were put in contact with the needs department. Social workers, who normally dealt with daily individual emergencies, staffed the needs department. Maintaining thorough records is an intricate part of all social work procedures. While trying not to create "red tape," social workers quickly mimeographed four differently colored information sheets with a separate color representing needs, resources, volunteers, and information inputs. These information sheets facilitated recording, matching needs with resources, and later follow-up studies.

Another group of volunteers which played an instrumental role in the center's operation was the AFL-CIO (UAW). The union's community service staff representative heard of the IEC operation on Tuesday and suggested to the president of the Wayne County AFL-CIO (UAW) Council that perhaps the union could provide a transportation service for the center. Tuesday evening the union contacted IEC and arrangements were made for the union to assume dispatching and transportation services. By contacting large firms in the Detroit area, the union was able to persuade companies to donate trucks and drivers so that an IEC transportation network could be developed. In addition to providing supervisory personnel, trucks and drivers, the union brought their own walkie-talkie communication setup. This setup provided an important source for internal communication and allowed for contact with drivers en route. With continual communication, drivers could be dispatched without ever having to report to the center. This arrangement not only saved time, but decreased confusion already present at the center.

*EDITOR'S NOTE: One professional social worker who came in at this point described her volunteer experiences to the IEC as follows: "Noise, activity and commotion pervaded the [Episcopal] Diocese office adjoining the Cathedral. Beautifully appointed offices had been taken over; the Bishop's office had become the command post. There was a wide variety of people; black and white, from clerics in white collars to very young girls in miniskirts. Many looked as if they hadn't slept all night and I think this was true. Slowly I began to recognize some faces. There were some workers from Central District Family Service. I saw Len Gordon and he explained roughly what was happening and took me to a meeting of the Interfaith Emergency Council. I left the meeting because I didn't think it was where I belonged. The Needs Section was manned by the social workers and handled calls for help. The Center worked on a twenty-four-hour basis for several days." FROM: "This Crucial Summer: The Interfaith Emergency Center," by Betty Kalichman, in *Update,* Detroit AJC Newsletter, December, 1967.

Not all volunteers were formally affiliated with community organizations. The main source of volunteers came from individual citizens who felt
they could help to alleviate the community's vast suffering. While many
volunteers spent only a short period at the center, a number of volunteers
stayed and formed a fairly stable volunteer core.

During the first evening of IEC operations, jobs were allocated in an
arbitrary manner. Individuals who came to the center were told to just pick
up a phone and start answering. As one individual stated, ". . . I wandered
into the Cathedral Center here on Woodward and said, 'Where can you use
me?' and they said, 'Sit there and answer the phone.' " Since tasks were not
defined, everyone did the same thing—answered telephones. However, as
types of incoming calls began to be classified a need arose for division of
labor.

Several persons who were present the first evening felt that if the other
men preferred organizing the operation, they would withdraw into the background and pick up some other aspects of the interfaith response (judicial
committee, long-range planning, financial donations, etc). One individual
who did withdraw into another area stated, ". . . we could see some of these
guys just loved to get in there and set up an organization and make it run
right and you know I would just as soon let somebody else do this who likes
to do it and not have to worry about it." Job assignments by personal preference was a major factor determining the eventual IEC leadership. Those who
decided to follow through with the IEC operation would eventually hold
leadership positions.

The basic organizational structure was superimposed early Tuesday
morning. After this initial structuring, tasks were allocated to volunteers
according to their particular skills or past experience. A primary example
of this was the allocation of the "needs" department to social workers. Because of previous experience in assessing individual needs over the telephone,
it was felt that social workers would have the necessary qualifications to
effectively organize a needs department. Departmental heads and other
leadership positions were also assigned according to an individual's organizational skills as assessed by the center's director. In a number of instances
volunteers would recommend friends who were particularly qualified to
handle certain tasks (*e.g.,* the switchboard operator was recommended because of her past experience as a Wayne State University operator).

Tasks were also allocated according to resources which the volunteers
possessed. Such was the case when the AFL-CIO (UAW) Wayne County
Council volunteered trucks and truck drivers to handle the dispatching and
coordinating of the overall transportation network. Their own independent
resources allowed the union officials to operate fairly autonomously, relying
on the rest of the organization only for information as to pick-up and de-

livery locations. In sum, task assignments occurred on the basis of arbitrary decisions, personal preference, past experience, and possession of a special resource.

In addition to receiving a large supply of volunteers, the IEC inherited a complex network of collection and distribution centers. With word out on Tuesday that IEC was operating, many suburban churches in Wayne, Oakland, Macomb, Washtenaw, and Ingham counties volunteered to collect food and clothing. Knowing both needs and resources, IEC was in the advantageous position to coordinate supply with demand. It established 25 collection centers and 21 distribution centers.

Other community organizations quickly heard of IEC efforts to coordinate a collection-distribution network and thought IEC the logical recipient for large quantities of material goods. One well-known food chain delivered a van containing five tons of canned goods, while a leading cereal company donated 11,000 cases of boxed cereal. IEC also received live shrimp, 70 cases of milk, a truckload of bread, food collected in Windsor (Ontario), as well as numerous other donations. A large parking lot adjacent to the center provided the needed space to divide and transfer food to trucks for delivery to distribution centers. While the bulk of material donated came from large companies, individual families gave food packages containing enough food for one other family.

General Responses in Summary

Although the major part of IEC activities involved supporting the collection and distribution network, calls from isolated and desperate individuals still kept coming into the center. Persons requesting food were referred to the distribution center closest to them, while those not able to get to a center were brought food by individual volunteers who made deliveries. Special volunteer teams made visits to persons calling in with special problems (*i.e.,* blindness, acute illness, fear, and so on). The police precinct station, located across the street, called upon IEC to aid in counseling National Guard personnel who, under the strain of the disturbance, were suffering from severe emotional stress.

As requests and resources continually were fed into the center, a number of reassessments and adjustments had to be made. The first major overall refinement occurred Tuesday morning when the center director superimposed a structure which basically would last for the entire emergency operation. Very little task distinctions existed the first evening of operations. However, on Tuesday because of a reassessment of phone calls, four distinct departments were formed, reflecting the type of requests and resources received. A needs department handled all calls from individuals requesting food or clothing, while a volunteer department was formed to process and assign volunteers to appropriate tasks. The resource department recorded all calls donating food, clothing, and other materials. This information was then passed on to a distribution department which matched needs with appropriate resources and dispatched trucks to make deliveries.

Once operations were underway, each department made a number of adjustments to increase efficiency and adapt to demands. Shortly after the needs department was formed refinements occurred in recording incoming calls. Information sheets were mimeographed to facilitate accurate record keeping.

The volunteer department also underwent a number of changes. After the call for volunteer aid went out over the mass media, volunteers were literally flocking to the center filling hallways and adding to the general confusion which already existed. One volunteer took it upon herself to organize a more efficient way of processing volunteers. It was decided to set up a registration desk at the one entrance to the center. Typed cards were then filled out for each volunteer to include name, address, special skills, family responsibilities, hours preferred. Volunteers were then selected according to their special skills and/or to the extent they could regularly report.

While departments had to adapt and refine their tasks, individual volunteers also refined tasks to increase efficiency. Small adjustments were made in record keeping, appropriate telephone responses, loading and unloading supplies, etc. These overall task adjustments provided a stabilized base from which the organization could develop.

Each volunteer answering calls continually made individual assessments and decisions which involved committing IEC resources to specific problem areas. The fact that everyone at the center was so involved in his own specific tasks deterred some volunteers from seeking consultation when making an important decision. However, in unusual or extremely difficult cases, decisions would be made by consulting co-workers or departmental heads. Callers donating perishable goods (*i.e.,* milk, butter, vegetables, etc.) were not accepted until volunteers consulted with department heads and other officers as to whether there would be adequate storage.

Decisions involving internal problems were often made in staff meetings held late at night or early morning. Calls started to slack off between midnight and 5:00 A.M. allowing time to plan the following day's activities as well as catch up on record keeping and sleep. It was at these late meetings that the only overt conflict arose. This conflict centered around deciding the appropriate time in which the center should phase out of its emergency activities. One faction felt that as soon as normal welfare agencies began to operate and take over the community welfare function that IEC should consider closing down its operation. From the start it was felt that the operation was only temporary. Others, however, felt that since so many persons had suffered either directly or indirectly that established welfare agencies would not and could not service everyone. The hardest hit by the disturbance were those individuals who were marginal—able to get along from week to week but vulnerable to any job disruption. It was these marginal individuals who mainly concerned those favoring extended IEC operations. These persons would suffer, since they technically were not eligible for welfare. Decision on phasing out IEC operations was continually postponed until finally a tacit agreement was reached. The center would exist as long as it was funded and/ or until there was no longer a demand for its services.

Phase Out

By Saturday, July 29, a plan had been developed to systematically phase out the food operations. A news release, given out at 11:00 A.M., explained the gradual phasing out of the distribution centers from 16, to 12, to 5, to 2 centers over a four-day period. A list was provided, naming each center and the closing date. From July 30 to August 4, the IEC went through a gradual dissolution. By Monday, July 31, the twelve individuals still working at the center realized that a whole new set of problems were emerging, directly related to the disturbance. Families who were separated from one another by arrests now sought to reunite themselves. Homeless families that had been taken in by friends or relatives during the disturbance were now obligated to find more permanent housing. And families who normally could make ends meet suddenly were faced with bills they were unable to pay because of the loss incurred during the disturbance. By Wednesday, August 2, there were only two trucks left which would transport food from donors to city-appointed and operated distribution centers. On Friday, August 4, the center was out of the food business and had technically phased out all emergency activity. However, the growing awareness of the continuing problems would again activate an interfaith response by reinstituting the center's activities in a different area.*

---

*EDITOR'S NOTE: While this discussion has only dealt with the initial development of IEC, in reality it existed until November 17, 1967. Between August 8 and September 1, the center focused its activity upon following up both the welfare cases initiated during the emergency period and the new cases that developed. During the period of September 1 and November 17, an effort was made to close all cases opened by the emergency center. Those that could not be closed by the center's staff were referred to existing social welfare agencies within the community. The IEC became the Interfaith Action Council (IAC) whose socially catalytic aims are noted in Gordon's article in part one.

The Post-Riot Period

The articles in part three consider the varying black and white communal and leadership responses to the racial cleavage in Detroit following the riot.

Given the socioeconomic predominance of whites generally and those in suburbia in particular, Donald Warren's analytic article offers valuable insights. Warren presents documentation of the social isolation, parochialism, and racial hostility that characterizes white suburban communities. The panic that enveloped whites in the riot aftermath was not, however, found to be equally intense in the nine suburban communities sampled nor among whites in Detroit. There is confirmation of the old thesis, presented by Lipset and others,[1] that lower social class status was associated with more fear and hostility toward Negroes than was found among upper socioeconomic whites. Yet, Warren found some major qualifications to this generally valid finding. Among Negroes social class did not affect the perception of the riot causes. Both riot area, largely low socioeconomic, and outer city, largely middle to upper-middle socioeconomic, Negro respondents coincided in their views that the riot was set off by the factors of "poor housing," "police brutality," and "lack of jobs." Upper-middle-class whites tended to agree on these factors, outlined in the Kerner Report, but this was significantly less so for those in suburban communities where the general climate of opinion was hostile toward the Negro community. In such areas the individuals of high status position tended to more closely parallel the lower status white perceptions that the causes of the riot were related to "teen-agers," "Black nationalism" and "too much welfare."

Whatever the immediate perceptions among whites in 1967 about the causes of the riot, Warren's descriptive term of *panic* is an accurate one. By 1968 panic among whites had subsided to the point that governmental, labor business, and other communal leadership began to build programmatic contacts with inner-city black leadership. Donald Lief's article describes the emergence of the New Detroit Committee in which "the leadership of the nation's fifth-largest city speaks a new language and operates with new rules." The conflicts that developed within and between the black and white communities are detailed in both Lief's and the *Detroit Scope Magazine* articles.

The last article by Mel Ravitz analyzes the crisis of Detroit as the crisis of all our cities. He points to the continuing racial conflict and to the areas of private and governmental action that can lead to accommodation. Ravitz stresses the point that

---

1. Seymour Martin Lipset, "Working Class Authoritarianism," *Political Man: The Social Bases of Politics* (New York: Anchor Books, 1963), pp. 87-126.

only a comprehensive community approach that includes educational, job training, low-cost housing, and other coordinated efforts offers any possibility of handling the vast scope of human problems in our urban areas.

The post-riot period in Detroit is characterized by the cumulative effects of the pre-riot community tension variables and the effects of the riot itself acting as an additional independent factor to continuing racial tensions. The ongoing crisis proportions of race relations in Detroit is succinctly reported by Hubert Locke in his evaluation of the July 1967 riot:

> The aftermath of the 1943 riot saw the city make its first real, albeit feeble, attempt to make racial integration and social progress a matter of public policy. The effects of the 1967 upheaval have had the opposite impact; not only has there been a significant polarization of black-white attitudes in the city, but a growing sense of estrangement and separation even between the liberal elements in each group. The theme in the black community in Detroit is currently that of self-help and self-determination; in those areas of the white populace where the mood is not one of outright hostility and repression, there is a pronounced feeling that whites must support black efforts but avoid involvement in black affairs.[2]

In essence the problematical state of race relations in Detroit, and the society at large, was stated in Martin Luther King's last book, *Where Do We Go From Here: Chaos or Community?*[3]

---

2. Hubert G. Locke, *The Detroit Riot of 1967* (Detroit: Wayne State University Press, 1969), p. 17.

3. Martin Luther King, Jr., *Where Do We Go From Here: Chaos or Community?* (New York: Harper and Row, Publishers, Inc., 1967).

Community Dissensus:
Black Militants and the
New Detroit Committee

Power Struggle Among the Black Militants

Detroit's most militant Negroes have rejected the leadership of the Reverend Albert Cleage Jr., have dumped him and are looking for a new leader.

These rock-hard militants helped kill the Federation for Self-Determination, headed by Cleage, and have gone "underground" until they find a new voice.

"I don't know anything about it. I suppose it's possible. But I don't believe there has been any change in my attitude" that would cause the militants to desert him, Cleage said.

When asked if he had heard reports that there was a price of $5,000 on his head, Cleage answered: "I read the reports; I've heard about them. But it ought to be much more than $5,000. Personal safety is not a factor to me—but I take measures to protect my safety."

The Federation, a corporation of about two dozen groups, represented some of Detroit's most hard-line black militants. It was dissolved and its funds—more than $1,200—were distributed to two ultra-militant organizations: The Inner City Voice newspaper and the Black Students Association at Wayne State University.

The death of the Federation stunned many blacks, who saw it as an effective force in Detroit's black ghettos. The dissolution may also open some eyes in the white community, which has reviled Cleage for what whites thought were his inflammatory urgings to the black community to pull apart from the whites—by violence, if necessary.

The black militants, however, look at Cleage through bitter eyes. They feel that in his contacts with the white community—first with the New Detroit Committee, more recently as a speaker before primarily white audiences—Cleage has moderated his views to the point where he no longer speaks for the militants.

From *Detroit Scope Magazine,* May 11, 1968.

"The black community needs any assistance possible," Cleage said, "including that from whites—without white domination. It must be a total effort to do what the black community wants done. No one in the black community cares if I talk to white groups. I'm concerned with building politically and building economically. I do what's necessary, and only time will tell if that's right."

One observer said: "The young militants have told Cleage to lay off (the whites), to have nothing to do with them." What has happened, he said, is unpublicized infighting in which both sides are trying to "eliminate the dissident elements."

Cleage recently cancelled a scheduled appearance at Royal Oak's First Baptist Church because of what he claimed were "pressures" from persons in that area.

"The type of phone calls and telegrams I have received from suburban citizens has convinced me that my appearance would only add to racial tensions in the suburbs," Cleage said in a telegram to the church explaining his absence.

"The benefits of going in and provoking an incident were not worth the risk," he added, while denying that the "pressure" had been applied by blacks instead of whites.

The executive director of Cleage's Citywide Citizens Action Committee, Edward Vaughn, was recently beaten and hospitalized.

When asked if the attack was connected to any split among black militants, Cleage replied: "I think there are psychopaths loose in any community."

The militants want nothing to do with those whites who talk, but take no action to change the system of white supremacy. These are the same people who feel that Cleage has not moved fast enough, or hard enough, to get what they want.

Cleage, on the other hand, has said such things as: "I don't have any particular interest in running up and down the streets throwing bricks . . . the rebellion I'm concerned about is the rebellion that gives black people control of the black community."

In the militants' eyes, the system is wrong, the system won't change. So the system must be destroyed.

Detroit's militant blacks don't talk about, or attack, each other in print. But one said: "The Federation was doomed from the start when it allowed Cleage to become chairman. He's a fiery speaker, but his inability as a politician led to the dissolution of the Federation."

The Federation was killed—one person who attended said "it was by an overwhelming vote; I don't remember any dissent"—at a meeting in the Fisher branch of the YMCA.

Most of the corporation's 50 individual members were present at the meeting, which was presided over by the group's vice-chairman, Lorenzo Freeman. He also is the director of the West Central Organization (WCO).

Among those attending were the board of directors, including chairman Cleage; Freeman; secretary Don Roberts, representing the Black Social Workers; Edgar Brazelton, a former Federation president who also is president of the Booker T. Washington Business Association; Dr. Orian Wordon, a professor at the University of Windsor; Frank Ditto, executive director of the East Side Voice for an Independent Detroit; and Dr. Karl Gregory, who was on leave as an assistant professor at Wayne State University to be the Federation's executive director.

Attorney Kenneth Cockrel, who is connected with the North Woodward Inter-Faith Project, made the motion to dissolve the Federation, acting on a recommendation made by the board of directors.

Cockrel's motion later was amended to provide that the dissolution would be permanent; and before it was approved, the board agreed on the distribution of unused funds.

Every member of the Federation who was representing another organization—many of them militant—had 10 votes. The at-large members (those representing only themselves) had one vote.

The reason given for the death of the Federation was that the individual militant groups wished to devote more time to their own projects.

One observer laid the blame for the Federation's failure at the doorstep of the New Detroit Committee for its purported failure to give the Federation money "without strings." He added that "the real militant movement in this community has gone back underground."

One young militant went even farther. He blamed the death of the Federation on the "lack of integrity and the personal ambitions of those who had the responsibility of making the Federation operative."

Both the Federation and the more moderate Detroit Council of Organizations (DCO) were formed shortly after last July's riots (militants call them rebellions) in Detroit, and both wanted the power to rebuild the inner-city black ghettos along their own lines.

The New Detroit Committee agreed to give Cleage's Federation a Ford Foundation grant of $100,000, but later postponed the decision when the DCO objected that the Committee was "trying to play God to the Negro community."

The Committee, caught in the middle, then offered $100,000 to both groups, each of which was to raise another $100,000. The money was to have been used for programs to make a start on rebuilding the ghettos.

The grant was accepted by the DCO, but angrily rejected by Cleage, who charged there were strings attached. Two of those strings were stipulations by the Committee that the two groups would cooperate, and would not use their money for politics.

Two Negro members of the Committee resigned after Cleage's rejection of New Detroit funds. One of them—Norvell Harrington—later returned to the Committee.

The real black militant power ultimately could fall along an axis connecting the Student Non-Violent Coordinating Committee (SNCC); the Black Students Association; and the Inner City Voice, whose editor, John Watson, heads what is considered to be the only militant press voice available to Detroit blacks.

Both SNCC and the Black Students have been bitterly critical of whites; Dan Aldridge, president of SNCC's Detroit chapter, says the white community doesn't know the black man, "can't possibly understand his problems, and can't do anything" for him.

One Negro spokesman said the power in Detroit's black community could increasingly fall to such elected officials as U.S. Rep. John Conyers, State Senator Coleman Young and Detroit Common Councilman Nicholas Hood.

Hood has become increasingly vocal lately, criticizing Mayor Cavanagh's budget for ignoring the needs of Detroit's lower-paid (Negro) workers, and charging the existence of discriminatory hiring practices at the Detroit Public Library.

But whether these elected officials—even recognizing that black votes helped put them where they are—can be militant enough to satisfy the demands of the militant "underground" remains to be seen.

No matter who grabs the power in the militant arena, Rev. Cleage will continue to speak through his Citizens Action Committee.

His voice will reach both black and white ears; but he will be tuned out by the most militant blacks.

The New Detroit Committee

Shiny black limousines carrying Detroit's industrial aristocracy whisper to the curb in front of the Detroit Bank & Trust Building a few days out of every month.

These smooth, white men stride up to the bank of elevators in the new shiny clean building and are whisked high up to suite 1515—where they convene, roll up their French cuffs, so to speak, and plunge elbow deep into the mucky, embarrassing problems of Detroit's black ghetto.

What's even more embarrassing than the squalor, rot and misery of the ghetto is the failure of these men, Detroit's most powerful men, acting as the New Detroit Committee, to get much done about it.

From the beginning, when the committee was established by September 1967 in response to Detroit's bloody insurrection, it has been widely predicted that the New Detroit Committee would fail to achieve meaningful improvements in the ghetto. The reasoning has been: White rich men can't understand and help the black poor.

In addition, the sincerity of the committee—formed by Gov. Romney and Mayor Cavanagh—has been questioned. Ever since the Civil War American politicians have been undercutting grassroots outbursts and demands for reform by setting up reform machinery without turning it on. The idea of those in power is to appease the discontented by pretending to do something about it.

In modern times the maneuver is to appoint a committee—either a study committee or an action committee—which must be given "sufficient time." Although there is often a great deal of sincere motivation for correction and progress in many cases, a lot of the intent is often just to quiet down protesters with consoling words and the appearance of doing something. Committees often turn out to be merely things that the Establishment can point to and say, "Take it easy. Be patient. We have a committee working on it."

There is a great deal of suspicion that the New Detroit Committee is that kind of committee—a move to appease the Negro community with the illusion that somebody is truly doing something about their problems, and thereby persuade them not to riot again. Any evaluation of the committee's achievements should include its success, if any, at calming the situation.

Is New Detroit turned on, tuned in? If so, where is it failing or succeeding? What's the outlook? Here are the answers:

The committee's recent progress report points ironically to one of its own major shortcomings. "Change," the report magisterially notes, "however well-planned or intended, cannot be achieved from without and above."

The committee's offices are on the 15th floor of the Detroit Bank and Trust Building, an ivory-colored tower of concrete on the corner of Fort and Washington Blvd. As for the makeup of the committee, a newsman says: "The membership list reads like awards night at Dun and Bradstreet." Henry Ford II . . . Lynn Townsend . . . James Roche . . . Walker Cisler. . . . This all qualifies as "without and above" the ghetto.

A New Detroit information officer defended the committee: "Sure it's a blue-ribbon committee because that's where the power is. But there are nitty-gritties too."

Of the 39 members selected by chairman Joseph L. Hudson Jr.,* only nine were Negroes. Three of these resigned—one in protest of the commit-

---

*EDITOR'S NOTE: Since this article was written in 1968, the New Detroit Committee has changed chairmen twice. In 1969 Max Fisher, a Jewish leader and business executive, and in 1970 William Patrick, a black leader and former Detroit Councilman, became chairmen respectively.

tee's method of dealing with the black militant Federation for Self Determination headed by Rev. Albert Cleage; another left town; the third resigned in the Cleage affair but returned later.

Only 17 of the 37 members actually live in Detroit.

The composition of the working staff has mixed blessings. Of 100 staffers only 15 are Negroes. With a handful of notable exceptions, the staffers are newcomers to ghetto problems. Dedicated and efficient, most staffers nonetheless came equipped with little more than textbook or cocktail party conceptions of what needs to be done. But education is swift, and no one is more committed than the newly converted. As one staffer—a public relations man on loan from an auto company—put it: "When I came here four months ago, I felt like a lot of other people: Why the hell don't these people do something for themselves? Now when I start talking about black babies getting their fingers chewed by rats, even my priest tells me to cool it."

The long-term benefits of such conversions are incalculable but good. Most of the borrowed staff members, whose salaries are paid by industry, take their new-found knowledge and social philosophy back to their jobs with them.

But can the committee afford on-the-job training of aides? U.S. Rep. John Conyers (D-Detroit) thinks not. "It's a little late for re-education," he snapped. "Where the hell have these people been all their lives?"

Conyers, a Negro, also seethes over what he contends is the total failure of the committee to deal with the single most inflammatory issue in the black community—white police. Noting the Kerner Commission's emphasis on this point, Conyers charged that New Detroit had failed totally to bring about improvement:

"Relations between the police and the black community are worse now than prior to July 23rd . . . it's not the same as the private community. When a bank clerk insults you, you go to another bank. Can you go to a different police department?"

New Detroit is aware of this failure: "(The) volatile relationship between the black community and the police is a fact of life in Detroit and . . . broad innovative change is imperative to remedying the situation."

The committee notes that its top priority project, a comprehensive review of the Detroit Police Department, proposed in September of 1967, never proceeded beyond the planning stage. The resignation of Commissioner Ray Girardin and the mayor's failure to find a successor, coupled with high costs of such a study, were given as reasons for shelving the project. Plans for police information centers in the ghetto likewise failed to get off the ground when the Common Council turned down the proposal despite New Detroit's backing.

The black community also chafes over the city's failure to recruit Negro police officers. Leon Atchison, one of Congressman Conyers' administrative assistants, put the number of Negroes on the Detroit force at 244, about five percent of the force's authorized strength.

"If enough Negroes can't meet the requirements," said Conyers, "then Detroit should do what Philadelphia did—pick up Negroes by the busload and teach them how to pass the tests."

But what, specifically, could New Detroit do to get movement on police-community relations?

"Put the heat on," Conyers suggested. "That's what all that power is supposed to be for."

Of necessity, the committee falls in the quasi-official twilight zone between government and private citizen. At the outset chairman Hudson warned that by seeming to take over the traditional roles of existing agencies or institutions, the committee might be mistaken as "a sort of supergovernment." To avoid this, it has limited itself almost exclusively to gentle urging.

But there have been exceptions. On April 23 the committee pledged nearly half a million dollars to fund two public school programs. $60,000 will go to the Highland Park Board of Education for a six-month project to woo 100 dropouts back into school for job training or preparation for higher education. $400,000 will go to the Detroit Board of Education to continue summer school education and job programs that would have gone under for lack of public funds.

The grants indicate that the committee is not unalterably wedded to its philosophy of mobilizing other agencies to do the job or raise the money. A committee spokesman explained: "We don't want to make a habit of it; we just don't have that kind of money for the massive effort needed. This was simply an emergency grant to keep Detroit from losing ground."

The committee, now established as a permanent agency with 127 concrete proposals as its goals, mostly long-term, has $2 million from the Ford Foundation, granted on a one-to-three matching basis. It does not, however, intend to be a funding agency.

New Detroit has gone a bit beyond the urging stage on open housing and tenant rights by going to Lansing to lobby at the Legislature.

The committee is also talking about taking off the velvet gloves in its efforts to get Negroes apprenticed in skilled trades. Despite the presence on the committee of Jack Wood, secretary-manager of the Detroit and Wayne County Building Trades Council, negligible progress has been made in placing Negroes in skilled apprentice programs. In February of 1966, for instance, there were 136 apprentices in the Ironworkers Union. None was a Negro. In February of 1968, there were 143 apprentices; only one was a Negro. The skilled trades unions say young Negroes simply aren't interested in the low rates paid apprentices and would prefer other jobs with less future but higher immediate rewards.

New Detroit is threatening to take the matter to court if significant progress is not made. But so far, it hasn't brought a case.

Another failure of the committee is in reaching the public. It says community attitudes need reshaping, but its contributions in this area have been negligible. A major problem has been the shutdown of Detroit's major newspapers. Even so, little has been done to encourage free-wheeling public discussion. The committee's sessions are held behind closed doors and the press is kept "informed" through infrequent and generally self-serving handouts.

Its major effort in shaping public attitudes has been the establishment of a speakers bureau that services Detroit and suburban church and civic groups. Through the bureau, the committee has reached more than 18,000 persons with its primary message: Civil rights is everybody's job and the problem is one of human dignity as much as housing jobs and education. It also has inaugurated a newsletter that ultimately will go to 10,000 community leaders and organizations, and the committee plans television forums and a documentary film for showing to private groups.

But the committee has reached only thousands when the audience it should be reaching numbers in millions.

New Detroit is concerned with the growing alienation between the white and Negro communities and admits it has been unable to reverse or even to halt the division. "The community," it points out, "is far from having been rebuilt, physically or socially. If anything, the conflict is in a more advanced state than it was in late July, 1967."

Of great concern is the increasing desire of private citizens to arm themselves. The committee lays this to "lack of understanding" between whites and Negroes and the spread of outrageous rumors about impending invasions, sniping and burning. The answer, New Detroit feels, is in "establishment of communications."

Congressman Conyers isn't convinced. "We talk about peace in the black community," he said. "What the hell, it's not the Negroes who are standing in line to buy guns."

His solution?

"Well, for one thing, Joe Hudson could close his gun shop."

New Detroit hasn't come up with anything better. Its progress report does not promote the need for gun control legislation, nor are there any other short-term proposals for cooling the present explosive gun situation.

In the area of education, neither the New Detroit Committee nor anyone else has been able to shake Lansing out of its lethargy on the need for massive state aid to the state's urban ghettos. In the wake of the July riot, the Detroit Board of Education asked the Legislature for $5.3 million in special emergency school aid. New Detroit put its imprimatur on the proposal and met with Gov. Romney. Romney requested an additional $5 million be placed into Section 4 of the State Aid Act—a formula which meant that Detroit would stand to receive only $2.3 million in added funds. The Legislature did not act on the proposal. Nor has it acted on a current request for $9 million for disadvantaged children.

New Detroit also has had continuing difficulty marshalling the support of black militants, many of whom consider any effort by whites a smoke screen—or worse, a plot.

"The committee has . . . supported and encouraged efforts by community organizations to provide 'grass roots' involvement in the physical and social restoration of the city."

That brief statement, appearing on page 66 of the progress report, represents New Detroit's greatest success and its greatest failure. It's greatest success has been in its dealings with the grass roots moderate organization, The Detroit Council of Organizations, headed by Rev. Roy Allen. New Detroit has given $100,000 to the DCO (to be matched by the Negro community through a fund-raising drive) and Rev. Allen's organization plans to launch into a promising program that will include a pilot project to:—involve citizens in monitoring, evaluating, and upgrading the performance of all schools within a single high school's district (yet to be picked)—expand job-training programs and strive to eliminate irrelevant job entry requirements—set up two Day Care and Child Development Centers as models for a citywide program designed to improve child care, parent skills and give parents an opportunity to take job training courses knowing their children will be properly cared for.

New Detroit's greatest grass-roots failure has been its inability to win support from the black militants. Some whites have expressed concern from the very first with New Detroit interest in the militants. They've found support from Negro leaders such as Whitney Young Jr., of the National Urban League, who has warned groups like New Detroit not to become "easy prey for racial racketeers—the charlatans in this business who try to blackmail businessmen."

New Detroit's members, however, realized from the start that militants are not necessarily racial racketeers. At the same time that it voted to offer $100,000 to Rev. Allen's organization, the committee offered $100,000 to Rev. Albert Cleage's Federation for Self Determination. Rev. Cleage, objecting to a New Detroit Committee requirement that a liaison man work between the federation and the committee, refused the money. He said that his group would not accept committee money if it meant committee control. The result was a stalemate. Neither side gave in and the federation disbanded.

Some black militants have scoffed at New Detroit from the beginning. A spokesman for the Student Non-Violent Coordinating Committee thinks there is only one purposeful action the committee can take.

"Disband," said Dan Aldridge, president of the Detroit chapter of SNCC. "The New Detroit Committee should just disband, take the money it has and give it to the black people.

"They (the committee members) ought to stop fooling themselves. The white middle class couldn't possibly understand the problems of the disenfranchised black man. They can not do anything for black people. They've just discovered us. How could they plan for us? I couldn't plan for them. I couldn't plan programs for Walker Cisler or J. L. Hudson if he were planning a store in the suburbs."

If New Detroit has a fatal flaw, it is, in Aldridge's view, that the committee speaks for the times only too well, times that he describes as "the present age of corporate imperialism." He charges that the committee itself manifests that imperialism and accuses it of representing "institutional racism," a concept its members have failed to recognize, according to Aldridge.

Institutional racism or no, Aldridge is not against accepting institutional money. "Institutional money is not white or black money," he said. "It's white AND black money. We pay taxes. In fact we pay taxes so white people can live in the suburbs. No one attempted to compensate us for the freeways. We don't use them. But they have taken up land and reduced our tax base."

If there is a good and proper role the New Detroit Committee can fulfill, Aldridge believes that role must be in dealing with white attitudes. "White people if they are sincere have to deal with other whites," he said. "An excellent program, for example, is PARA (People Against Racism, an all-white group concerned with changing attitudes of the white community, especially in the suburbs).

If attitudes are to be changed, channels of communication must be opened and unrestricted dialog flow through them. That has not been the case and Aldridge blames the most personal medium of all—television. Its effect, he contends, has been to make things worse.

"White people stick together and they're killing us every day," he said. "The Indians lose the 11 o'clock movie. The black people lose the 6 o'clock news."

He pointed out that there is not one television series dealing with the life of a black man as he lives it. For what comfort it may be to Aldridge, NBC has apparently given in a little. It is carrying a series starring Diahann

Carroll, a program about the life of a black working woman, a program intended, the network has promised, to tell it like it is.

Congressman Conyers' aide Leon Atchison agreed that the Negro's image on television has been distorted, even omitted. Referring to commercials, he said: "You'd think Negroes don't brush their teeth or use soap. We need more Negroes seen in normal roles." Here Atchison was repeating an oft-heard criticism by Negroes, that the few black actors who are in the business never play real-life roles. Instead, those like Sidney Poitier and Bill Cosby play "Supernigger," as evidenced by "In the Heat of the Night" (Poitier, a supercop, shows a small town southern white police chief how to catch a killer) and "I Spy" (Cosby ranges through exotic lands playing a superspy). "How many Bill Cosby's do you see on the street?" asked Atchison.

Whether a project to help the ghetto is run by New Detroit or by a black group, the point is that projects are in themselves quite necessary. Aldridge admitted this, pointing out that from a practical standpoint, someone has to know how to distribute the money. One of the prevailing puzzles in the minds of whites has been whom to give the money to. Are there black leaders? Do the leaders have programs? Will they have programs?

Rev. Cleage promises that he is pushing for them. In fact, in his view, if black people want to overcome white racists, they must "outprogram them."

In a column written in the *Michigan Chronicle,* Cleage suggested that if the black people were 90 percent of the population, they could merely walk over white oppressors. However, because they are only 10 to 15 percent of the population, "We can't do it by walking over white folks. We have to outthink them. We have to out-structure them. We have to outprogram them. . . . We are not waiting for instant integration. Nor are we waiting for instant Armageddon. That means we have to structure a different kind of program."

Cleage is not as militant as some black power advocates nor as mild as the Negro groups that favor integration. If he is to be classified as anything, it would be as a spokesman for black self-determination.

Probably the one point of agreement between separatist Cleage and integrationist Rev. Roy Allen is the need for good programs and a fair share of white money to support them. While New Detroit has apparently made money available, it has not acted swiftly to apply it where needed, to invest in the ghetto. Perhaps the fault is simply that it as a committee suffers the malady of all committees—turtle reaction time.

In other cities and even in Detroit, progress, albeit small, has been made to bypass the all-things-in-due-time committee system and to promptly bring investments in business and housing back into the ghetto.

In Cleveland, Warner & Swasey has contributed to both basic needs. It has already provided the funding for rehabilitating a low-cost housing project in that city's dismal Hough ghetto and then at cost turned the keys over to Cleveland authorities. Dr. James C. Hodge, president of W&S, announced that the company was starting up a small manufacturing concern to be called Hough Manufacturing Co., Inc. W&S is starting it in a 30,000-square foot building in the Wade Park area and will help train the initial 50 employes to compete in the manufacture of pallets, storage containers, and hydraulic fittings. Black personnel will manage and eventually own the new company.

In the Watts section of Los Angeles, Aerojet-General Corporation has founded a tent manufacturing company to work toward many of the same goals. Providing an initial 450 jobs, the company—Watts Manufacturing—was swamped by 5,000 job seekers.

In Newark, the Prudential Life Insurance Company paid for a $4.5 million co-operative housing project bordering the 1967 riot area.

In Chicago, the U.S. Gypsum Company is rehabilitating six slum tenements (150 apartments) at a cost of $1.8 million.

In Pittsburgh, 19 corporations formed the Allegheny Housing Rehabilitation Corporation and kicked in $1.4 million to buy and renovate ghetto houses and sell them back to ghetto residents.

In New York, IBM is starting up a 300-worker computer cable factory in Brooklyn's Bedford-Stuyvesant slums.

In Detroit there are some signs of action in the business community: The auto companies have all launched programs to hire the previously unhireable workers, most from the inner city. There is some effort in the field of housing as the Campbell Group builds four apartment houses on 12th Street; it is working on a non-profit basis, attempting through innovative construction methods to put up the project for $10 a square foot, well under the usual $16 to $20 per square foot cost. The result will mean new apartments will be available to ghetto residents at more reasonable prices. J. L. Hudson himself has acted faster than his committee. In November 1967 his department store launched a program to hire and train 250 hard-core unemployed persons and 250 students who might be considered potential dropouts.

In both major areas, jobs and housing, however, New Detroit has failed to induce big investment. Compared to the significant efforts made privately in other cities to bring industry back to the ghetto and to permit black men to operate it, own it, and profit from it, Detroit, the citadel of private enterprise, has been among the least enterprising of all. Regrettably, the committee may have acted as a brake upon private projects. Enterprising businessmen who might have acted on their own (in the absence of such a committee) have failed thus far to act, waiting for New Detroit to say when and where.

That the committee means to accomplish much in these areas is clear. In its own statement of purposes, it reports in section 19 A: "The New Detroit Committee in the field of housing (should) continue to make its support available to the Metropolitan Detroit Citizens Development Authority as the principal means of creating new and rehabilitated low income housing."

And in section 23 A: "The New Detroit Committee in the field of Economic Development (should) work with the city administration to encourage employers to locate within the inner-city . . . (and) offer facilities for financing and management counseling for firms interested in locating within the inner-city."

But when, New Detroit? And where?

Conclusions

New Detroit has recognized many of the problems of Negroes but it has failed to take much action. It has particularly failed to set up immediate, short-range programs that the urgency of the racial crisis demands. While the committee is on the right track in areas such as improving police-Negro relations, it has failed to use its full economic-social-political power to push through such programs. At the same time, the Mayor and the Governor have resisted programs suggested by their own committee, and this leaves in doubt their true purpose for establishing New Detroit. If part of their purpose was to calm the ghetto with appearances, the committee appears to be failing in that respect too. The Negro community is aware of its failures. More resentment, rather than less, may be the result.

Community Dissensus: Panic in Suburbia

Donald I. Warren

Whitney Young's recent call for social research in the White community further underscores the need to advance the analysis central to the Kerner Commission Report on Civil Disorders. The impetus for such efforts is particularly great in the Detroit Metropolitan area due to widespread anxiety of whites and blacks coupled with a dirth of information flow across community boundaries. This condition has resulted in a further spiraling of tensions. Much of what occurs represents the "self-fulfilling" prophesies of extremist groups—white and black. While efforts to break into this vicious circle of distrust are numerous, no systematic effort at coordination has been undertaken nor is likely to occur. Suburban communities where "white racism" is fostered or opposed are stereotyped as monolithic entities. Messages to the black community are weak or ineffectual on the ameliorative side, potent on the exacerbative side. What we have sought is to assess the overall scene and provide a better means of understanding what is occurring in white suburban areas. *Our concern is not a study of racist attitudes per se. Rather, the key requirement is an evaluation of perceptions and the climate in which they are developed.*

The Detroit "Scene"—1967-68

At the outset it is necessary to set the backdrop of events from the last week in July of 1967 to the time nearly one year later that this study was conducted. The Kerner Report devotes some 24 pages to a description of what occurred in Detroit between the evening of July 22 and July 30.[1] Forty-

---

Based upon a paper presented at the 64th Annual Meeting of the American Sociological Association, San Francisco, California, September 1969. The author is in the College of Social Work, University of Michigan. This article is previously unpublished.
1. The Kerner Commission does not provide an injury estimate. However *Newsweek* magazine on August 7, 1967, reported 2,250 injuries. The Kerner Commission report indicates that of 27 persons charged with sniping, 22 had charges against them dismissed. Chapter 1, section VIII, of the report is replete with testimony and incidents of mistaken sniper activity and identity.

three persons were killed, 33 black and 10 white. Action by police accounted for 20 deaths. Action by the Army for one. Store owners shot two others. Damage estimates originally set as high as $500 million were quickly scaled down. Later figures put the loss closer to $50 million.

In the aftermath of this last week of July charges of dalliance, inefficiency, and mishandling of the riot situation were leveled at local, state, and federal officials. Of particular concern was the widespread recognition that the entrance of the National Guard units contributed to the confusion and violence of the riot and was officially underlined by a special presidential envoy to Detroit, Cyrus Vance in his famous reference to "trigger-happy" Guardsmen.[2] Certainly the 1943 riot experience was thought to have provided a means for coordinating governmental action. But 1967 brought a total sense of dismay that permeated the whole Detroit community—both black and white. The basic question was "What had happened to a liberal and progressive community?"

Attempts to provide a "definition of the situation" at first focused on the disorders: (1) Both white and Negro looters were present in riot areas and were often described as "buddy-buddy" by Negro residents; and (2) Spontaneous white hostility or retaliation against Negroes, as reported in 1943, was absent.[3]

On July 28 the *Detroit Free Press* bannered a story, "Experts Rule Out Racism." The story quoted a political scientist: "There has not been the racism in this riot that was true for example in Watts."[4] The editorial in the same paper stated:

Two philosophical attitudes have in recent years been moving across the country . . . a parental and individual permissiveness and an official permissiveness that have left a slackness and a fuzzing of responsibilities. . . .[5]

The theme of a lawless atmosphere was echoed by many white and Negro leaders over the following days. The mayor of Highland Park, an enclave near the riot zone, said, "A show of force would have helped the situation immeasurably . . . I do not think a majority of the people, including Negroes, wanted to let the looting go on as promiscuously as it did."[6] A Negro minister stated:

2. *Detroit Free Press,* July 28, 1967.
3. The common belief that the 1943 riot was primarily one of whites attacking Negroes is based on two factors: (1) The absence of Negro journalists who could closely observe the initial hostility and organization of Negroes, and (2) The popularity of A. M. Lee's and N. R. Humphrey's book, *Race Riot* (New York: Dryden Press, 1943). A far superior effort is the recent account of R. Shogan and T. Craig, *The Detroit Race Riot* (Philadelphia: Chilton Books, 1964).
4. *Detroit Free Press,* July 28, 1967.
5. Ibid.
6. Detroit *News,* July 29, 1967.

There are not only privileges but responsibilities in civil rights. The Negro people must accept this area of responsibility. The few do not want to accept it. . . . [7]

A statement issued on July 25 by "100 Negro leaders" declared:

The great majority of Detroit's 550,000 Negroes deplore and condemn lawlessness, hoodlumism . . . of the non-thinking among us.[8]

One leader in the labor field stated that "the burning and looting were the work of a disorganized criminal element."[9] Another comment was that "There was nothing racial . . . there were more Negroes because it happened in a Negro domain. . . ."[10] The first day of the disorder, a Negro Congressman said, "The crowd was fused with alcohol and drugs."[11] Detroit's only Negro Councilman stated the same day, "The rioters are a completely lawless group that must be controlled."[12] The third day of the disorder a *Detroit Free Press* editorial commented:

This is not Negroes against 'Whitey'—a hoodlum uprising became a riot and then integrated anarchy as Negro looters were joined by whites and Guardsmen were joined by Negro vigilantes. . . . The time has come in the civil rights movement to draw finer and clearer lines . . . to separate . . . the basically good people . . . from the hoods and the punks. Hoodlums, whatever their color, must be separated from society.[13]

The same paper, on August 6, described the work of Negro peacemakers on 12th Street. One of those persons, the Congressman from the district, had retreated from an effort to speak to the crowds in the streets. He said later, "There is nobody. Nobody to talk to out there. Everyone who is worth talking to is in their homes."[14]

As the events of July moved into the interpretations of August, the view of rioters as a lawless element—a tiny minority of the Negro population—began to be structured in two directions: (1) the role of outside agitators and (2) economic deprivation as the riot cause. Soon, however, statements by public officials, including FBI spokesmen, discounted the idea that outside agitators were involved. The "poverty" theory was a logical outgrowth of the view of rioters as uneducated, unemployed, young, and delinquent. One statement by a Negro school administrator typified this view:

7. Detroit *News,* August 1, 1967.
8. Detroit *Free Press,* July 25, 1967.
9. Ibid.
10. Ibid.
11. Detroit *News,* July 24, 1967.
12. Ibid.
13. Editorial, Detroit *Free Press,* July 25, 1967.
14. Detroit *Free Press,* August 6, 1967.

The 12th Street area is one of the worst trouble spots in the city with high unemployment, juvenile delinquency, slum crowding, and wide open crime and prostitution.[15]

The editor of a suburban Detroit newspaper wrote:

The . . . disorders . . . were the have-nots against the haves, and against the city and the authority of the city. They were against the city because that's where the urban poor are concentrated. They were not mass movements but the actions of the few.[16]

President Johnson's address to the nation on the evening of July 27 gave further support to the poverty theory. This was a persistent theme; it was echoed nearly a month later by the Negro community newspaper in its editorial August 19:

No matter how well one explains away *why* they are have-nots—lack of education, inability to learn, laziness, disadvantagement, etc.—the fact remains that they have not and they are fed up with that status in life.[17]

But paramount to the theme of poverty was the sense that the Detroit disorder was not part of the civil rights movement. As one citizen said, "It's not civil rights and it's not racial. It's just people that want something for nothing. They just want to steal."[18] A similar view was voiced by a Negro minister whose church is in the immediate riot area:

There is some nasty slang on the surface, but deep down it's a mess created by people who won't work. I would discourage [*sic*] this type of thing, but unfortunately we created this thing, by raising up youngsters, many on ADC . . . who are not grateful for anything.[19]

Such a view also links poverty to a generational conflict. A persistent topic for commentary was the young hoods and delinquents:

Was it a civil rights explosion? Perhaps in the very broadest sense. The street corner loungers who gathered . . . to heckle police as they cleaned out a blind pig; the toughs who transformed a crowd into a mob by smashing windows; the looters who exploited the opportunity; all these can be called the product of past generations of injustice. But these mobsters, arsonists, and looters were not fighting a civil rights battle.[20]

In this first stage of definition both white and Negro leaders tended to take similar public views of what had happened. What separated the public

15. Assistant Superintendent Detroit Schools, in the Detroit *News,* July 24, 1967.
16. Editorial, Royal Oak *Daily Tribune,* July 26, 1967.
17. Editorial, *Michigan Chronicle,* August 19, 1967.
18. Negro citizen interviewed on the street, reported in Detroit *News,* July 25, 1967.
19. Negro minister, Rev. C. Williams, quoted in Detroit *Free Press,* July 24, 1967.
20. Editorial, Detroit *News,* July 24, 1967.

debate in the white and Negro communities appeared less important than what bound them together: a mutual sense of surprise, a recognition that "an underclass"[21] had been responsible, and that this was the work of a small minority, fed by criminal elements.

As the year 1967 drew to a close, the specter of black militancy loomed large in the media coverage in the Detroit Metropolitan area. Rap Brown had spoken in the riot area in August and was quoted as saying that "Negroes should stop looting and start shooting." When the New Detroit Committee was formed nine of its 39 members were Negro—three from militant ghetto organizations. In September, J. L. Hudson, Chairman of NDC, held a press conference at which Rev. Albert Cleage announced the accord of his newly formed Citizens City Wide Action Committee with Hudson. The goal of the group was indicated by Cleage to be self-determination and "the transfer of power to the Black Community."

In November, Detroits' two large daily papers were struck and ceased functioning until the summer of 1968. In January of 1968, the leader of a moderate Negro group had his home firebombed. Two Negro businesses were firebombed in February. The April assassination of Dr. King required the imposing of a tight curfew on Detroit along with the use of the National Guard.

Thus did the white suburbanite greet the prospect of a "long hot summer" in Detroit. That spring was sprinkled liberally with reports of soaring gun sales and the creation of a rumor clinic to dispel fears of black militants invading the suburbs to kill white children. This latter concoction was refuted by a local TV commentator who invited a separatist leader to "dispel" this allegation on his program. The era of the ritual black-white confrontation on the media had reached its height in Detroit—tensions appeared to also.

The Suburban Sample

In May of 1968, a panel of respondents was selected from telephone directories in nine communities surrounding Detroit. The resulting group of communities reflect a wide geographic band spanning the northeast to the southwest: They circumscribe the city of Detroit—this often being referred to in the black ghetto as the "White Noose."

Appendix Table A indicates the population size and growth which has been occurring in the selected communities. Data taken from a report of the Southeast Michigan Council of Governments indicates better than a one-third increase in size occurred between 1960 and 1967. Communities such

21. Daniel P. Moynihan stressed this term on the NBC Television Special on the Detroit riot "Summer 1967" on September 15, 1967.

as Southfield and Warren have doubled in population during the same period. By contrast, the population of both Dearborn and East Detroit have remained almost stationary. At the time of the Detroit riot of July 1967 the total population of the nine communities under study was estimated at more than two-thirds of a million persons. This represents about one out of every six persons in the tri-county S.M.S.A. Despite the variations between communities noted in Appendix Table A, we find one very stable characteristic of the satellites examined: They are totally white. The highest level of non-white population is less than one-half of 1%. Without doubt we are representing in our analysis a separate white world.

The communities we have selected are composed of young and growing families. The life of these communities is one focused on child rearing. With one or two exceptions, households without children represent less than one-third of all households in their community.

Because our analysis required an economical and efficient means to compare communities, we employed the telephone directory lists of households and drew names at random using an interval based on the goal of a one-half of 1% sample of the 186,500 dwelling units. We employed a base of 100 respondents for the smaller communities and 200 for the larger. With a total sample of 1150 households this meant an original sample fraction of slightly over six-tenths of 1% in the nine communities. Although there is some bias in the use of a telephone book sample, the danger of greatly distorting the profile of a suburban community is reduced compared to the central city. The Literary Digest fiasco* (so frequently cited as a classic bias in sampling techniques) is less applicable to an affluent suburban society where owning a telephone is taken for granted.

To check on any bias we have presented the socio-economic characteristics of the respondents in our sample in comparison to the systematic estimates of the Traffic and Land Use Study (TALUS) conducted in 1965-66 (see Appendix Table B). Given a slight bias towards returns from the more affluent and better educated (coupled with the improvement in the standard of living) we find our sample has more high income and better educated members than the community at large. However if we examine the occupational distribution for our sample and the 4% TALUS sample we find very comparable patterns.

Appendix Table C shows the response rate for the nine communities presented. Questionnaires were mailed out during May and contacts by telephone followed. Where possible, the individual was asked to complete the questionnaire on the telephone. Of the 788 completed forms, 287 were

*EDITOR'S NOTE: Using a sample of their upper and upper-middle class subscribers the Literary Digest predicted a landslide victory for Landon over Roosevelt in the 1936 presidential election.

obtained in this manner. Where personal interviews in the home are employed, completion rates may range from 70% to 90% and are generally centered at the 80% level. Given the failure to contact individuals because of household movement, vacation absences, and other reasons leading to non-completion of questionnaires, the level of success in the study is actually underestimated in Appendix Table C. If the proportion of completed questionnaires for persons actually contacted is employed, the overall response rate is approximately 77%. *Given this degree of potential error in representing the satellite communities it is important to focus on relative differences between communities not on percentages for given communities as absolute predictors.*

Hypothesis Basic to This Study

Our concern in collecting information from nine communities is not simply to study communities as such. Nor is it to find out the attitudes of individuals. Neither perspective is useful unless the two elements are put together. Individuals do not live in isolation from their fellows nor do communities have identical inhabitants. Stereotypes do nothing but prevent us from studying the true facts of a situation. Three key ideas seek to carry us beyond simply an analysis of atomized units:

1. Events in the world are defined and changed by the ideas people have about them. The Detroit riot created a perception which becomes more important than the original events of the rioting.
2. People are affected by their perceptions and attitudes when they take action—whether it be voting or joining groups or purchasing firearms. It is not enough to understand attitudes but these must be placed in the context of behavior. At the same time, behavior must be linked to pre-existing attitudes and perceptions.
3. The climate of opinion in a community affects what people think and do apart from what the same individual might think or do if he lived in a different community. This means that the community milieu has a powerful effect on individuals regardless of their background or point of view.

All of these propositions have direct relevance to the race situation in Detroit suburbs. What we hope to do in our analysis is to describe the manner in which these patterns manifest themselves.

Riot Anxiety

The first area tapped in the suburban questionnaire was the extent of anxiety about racial disorders in Detroit. We phrased such an inquiry in terms of a projective question: "Considering the neighbors and the people you know, how concerned would you say they are about the likelihood of new racial disorders in the coming months?" Table 1 contains the response for each of the nine communities. Overall, 1 in 2 suburbanites saw his peers

TABLE 1

CONCERN ABOUT NEW RACE DISORDERS
FOR THE SATELLITE COMMUNITIES

	Percent "very concerned"
Southgate (BC) †	58.2%
Southfield (WC)	54.2
Livonia (WC)	53.2
Royal Oak (WC)	49.5
Dearborn (WC)	49.2
East Detroit (BC)	43.5
Warren (BC)	43.5
Madison Heights (BC)	42.0
Plymouth (WC)	38.3
Total	47.8% (N=788)

†Majority of families in the community are blue-collar (BC) or white-collar (WC).

"very concerned" about future riots. We note that differentials between communities are pronounced. Of the five highest anxiety communities four are predominantly white-collar suburbs. Thus, following months of conditioning the suburbs entered the summer of 1968 with a clear case of the jitters.

To more specifically measure the race tension of white suburbs we built into the question a five-item cluster of behavioral items focused on actions in response to race fears. These items in turn were used to construct an index of community tension. Included were these five actions: (1) contacting police about riot dangers, (2) attending meetings on riot dangers, (3) reading pamphlets about protection against riots, (4) purchasing firearms to use in the event of riots, and (5) training in the use of firearms. In regard to this latter item several "gun clinics" had been established in Detroit suburbs so that housewives or others could have "proper" training since they had already decided to buy firearms.

Table 2 indicates how suburbanites perceived their peers in regard to purchasing guns. About 1 in 4 respondents indicated that at least "some" of his friends or neighbors were buying guns. This figure is 3 out of 5 if we include responses of a "a few" friends or neighbors buying guns. Table 2 indicates important differences *between* suburbs. In contrast to Table 1, blue-collar communities are highest in expressing race tension. When the other less hostile tension items are employed we find that white-collar communities react more in terms of intellectual anxieties—*i.e.,* attending meetings, reading, or merely "hand-wringing."

TABLE 2

PERCEPTION OF NEIGHBORS AND FRIENDS
"PURCHASING FIREARMS TO PREPARE
FOR RIOT DANGERS"

	Percent Indicating "Some" or "Many" Neighbors Taking This Action
Southgate (BC)†	37.7%
Dearborn (WC)	29.4
Warren (BC)	28.5
East Detroit (BC)	27.4
Madison Heights (BC)	26.7
Southfield (WC)	26.0
Livonia (WC)	22.6
Plymouth (WC)	22.2
Royal Oak (WC)	21.4
Average	26.8% (N=788)

†Majority of families in the community are blue-collar (BC) or white-collar (WC).

Table 3 summarizes the riot tension pattern of Detroit suburbs. Although our dichotomization into "high" and "low" is utilized here and in subsequent tables, it is clear that a somewhat more descriptive labeling would be to refer to communities as "very high" versus "medium high." In any event the dividing point employed serves as our indicator of community climate.

TABLE 3

RIOT TENSION CLIMATE RATING OF DETROIT
SATELLITE SUBURBS

Community	Average Percent on Five Indicators* of Perceived Neighbor Riot Reactions	Rating
Southgate (BC)†	35.4%	High
East Detroit (BC)	32.8	High
Dearborn (WC)	32.4	High
Warren (BC)	30.8	High
Southfield (WC)	30.7	High
Plymouth (WC)	27.6	Low
Livonia (WC)	27.4	Low
Madison Heights (BC)	26.8	Low
Royal Oak (WC)	24.6	Low
Average	29.8% (N=788)	

*The items included are: (neighbors and friends active)
  a. Contacted their police force about possible danger.
  b. Purchased firearms to prepare for dangers.
  c. Taken training in the use of firearms.
  d. Read pamphlets about protection against riot dangers.
  e. Attended meetings concerned about riot dangers.
†Majority of families in the community are blue-collar (BC) or white-collar (WC).

Perceived Riot Causes

Using the explanations prevalent in the media as bases for perceptions of suburbanites to the Detroit disorders, the following question was posed:

People have different ideas on what caused the disorders in Detroit last summer. Which of the following do you think is the most important reason that the disorders occurred?

Table 4 summarizes the responses which were given in the satellite communities. Since a first, second, and third cause could be indicated, percentages greatly exceed 100%. Notable in the list of perceived riot causes are the elements of the "riffraff" theory and the "conspiracy theory." In the first conceptions, rioters are seen as the unemployed, the criminal, the indolent or the irresponsible teen-ager. Of the suburban respondents, about 1 in 4 picked the "riffraff" theory as a first choice explanation. More than 1 in 3 picked economic deprivations—poor housing, lack of jobs, or simply poverty. An-

other 1 in 5 respondents attributes the riot to the influence of black nationalists. Less than 1 in 100 suburbanites sees police abuse or behavior as a riot
cause. One in 12 respondents views Negro powerlessness as the riot cause.
*For the vast majority of persons in satellite communities the Detroit riot was
as likely to be the work of social undesirables or agitators as it was to be
attributed to more enduring social forces.*

TABLE 4

ORDERING OF RESPONSES TO 10 CAUSES OF THE
1967 DETROIT DISORDERS FOR ALL SATELLITE
COMMUNITIES

"Which of the following do you think is the most important reason that the disorders occurred?"

	First-Choice Responses	Total First-, Second-, and Third-Choice Responses
Black Nationalism	16.0%	40.5%
Poverty	15.7	37.5
Criminal Elements	10.8	31.2
Lack of Jobs	9.1	31.7
Failure of White Public Officials	7.0	25.6
Powerlessness	6.9	20.8
Poor Housing	6.7	25.4
Too Much Welfare	6.6	26.0
Teen-agers	4.7	24.6
Police Brutality	0.7	3.1
Don't know	10.8	—
Other	4.1	—
Not ascertained	1.0	—
	100.1% (N=788)	

Because we have employed a similar list of riot causes in surveys in Detroit, it is possible to compare the suburbanite's view of the Detroit riot with
that of the white or black inhabitant closer to the scene. Appendix Table D
presents such information. In three studies in the Negro community, we find
a rank order of riot causes substantially different from that drawn up by
white suburbanites. In particular, the role of police abuses shows a totally

reversed perspective for black Detroiters. Black Nationalism, teen-agers, and welfare indolents are seen in the eyes of such middle-class Negroes to be unrelated to the riot. By starting from such radically different perspectives on the Detroit disorders it is easy to imagine the other bases for misperception between the white suburbs and the black ghetto.

One of the prime questions raised in our analysis of riot perceptions and civil rights priorities is the theory that behavior is *situationally determined*. This means that people proceed from the most immediate to the more distant. Civil rights goals are general and diffuse. The riot was specific, near, and dramatic. It demands explanation. It provokes a sense of incomprehension. To fill this vacuum in understanding, perceptions are developed and sustained by contact with like-thinking neighbors and friends. In this sense a climate of opinion emerges to define what the riot is about and what produced it. Such a view requires that we examine how *communities* perceive events. Table 5 presents such an analysis, using rankings for riot causes common to studies in Detroit and the present population of suburbanites. The patterns shown measure how similar are the perceptions of a given community with middle-income Negroes surveyed at about the same point in time. We note that satellite communities—with the exception of the police brutality issue—differ in their rankings of riot causes. These differences are not substantial. However, we can order the nine communities in terms of their *"perceptual distance"* from Detroit middle-income Negroes. Using this approach we can speak of the communication gap between suburbs and the black ghetto. When the rank ordering on riot tension is correlated with the measure of "perceptual distance," the Spearman coefficient is –.865—*showing a significant inverse relationship between a communities' fear of new disorders and its shared perceptions with their black socioeconomic peers in Detroit.*

Community Climate and
the Kerner Report

In March of 1968 the findings of the Kerner Commission were released. Because of the newspaper strike the impact of the findings about police abuses and media distortion did not have great circulation. Of the total sample 19.2% indicated they had or were reading the report. The correlation between the percent of readers and community riot tension is –.185—indicating some tendency for low-tension suburbs to have more Kerner Report readers.

Table 6 indicates how white suburbanites perceived the eight suggested findings of the Kerner Report. Some of the possible conclusions listed were clearly refuted by the report. The two closest to the basic finding are those

TABLE 5

NINE SUBURBANITE COMMUNITIES IN RELATION TO PERCEPTIONS OF THE 1967 RIOT SHARED WITH DETROIT NEGROES

(Communities arranged by the increasing amount of difference with Detroit Negroes)

	Detroit Middle-Income Negro Survey (May 1968)	Plymouth	Madison Heights	South-field	Royal Oak	Livonia	Dear-born	Warren	South-gate	East Detroit
Police Brutality	(1)	(8)	(8)	(8)	(8)	(8)	(8)	(8)	(8)	(8)
Poor Housing	(2)	(2)	(3)	(6.5)	(4)	(4)	(4)	(5.5)	(4)	(6)
Lack of Jobs	(3)	(1)	(4.5)	(3)	(3)	(3)	(3)	(3)	(3)	(7)
Poverty	(4)	(3.5)	(1)	(3)	(1)	(2)	(2)	(2)	(2)	(3.5)
Disappointment with White Public Officials	(5)	(3.5)	(7)	(5)	(7)	(7)	(7)	(5.5)	(6.5)	(2)
Teen-agers	(6)	(7)	(6)	(6)	(5)	(5)	(6)	(7)	(5)	(5)
Black Nationalism	(7)	(5)	(2)	(1)	(2)	(1)	(1)	(1)	(1)	(1)
Too Much Welfare	(8)	(6)	(4.5)	(7)	(6)	(6)	(5)	(4)	(4)	(3.5)

regarding built-in racism and the rejection by Negroes of separatism. What Table 6 clearly indicates is that only 1 in 5 suburbanites correctly perceived the major finding on racism—while the most frequently cited conclusion—that the police were too weak—was elaborately refuted in regard to the Detroit disorders. Another explicitly rejected analysis by the Kerner Commission was the role of militants. Yet as many suburbanites see militants causing riots as those who see racism as the source of racial disorders.

TABLE 6

ORDERING OF RESPONSES TO EIGHT SUGGESTED CONCLUSIONS
OF THE PRESIDENT'S COMMISSION ON CIVIL DISORDERS

"Which of the following do you consider the most important conclusion of the President's Commission on Civil Disorders—The Kerner Commission Report?"

	Percent Selecting the Response (More than one choice could be made)
Police Control of Riots Is Too Weak	33.5%
Few Negroes with Even Moderate Income or Education Participated in Rioting	21.7
WHITES HAVE CREATED A BUILT-IN RACIST SYSTEM*	19.6
Militant Groups Caused the Riots	19.3
Negroes Are Better Off Than Ever Before	15.6
MOST EGROES BELIEVE THAT SEPARATION IS FOOLISH*	5.9
Large Federal Programs Will Solve Race Problems	5.2
The Solution to the Race Situation Is Hopeless	3.1

*These alternatives come closest to actual conclusions of the Kerner Report.

In terms of reading of the Kerner Report it was not surprising to find that the college-educated respondents were more likely to have read it than noncollege respondents. However some community climate impact was apparent. Table 7 contains the relevant findings. College-educated respondents living in low riot tension communities are somewhat more likely to have read the Kerner Report than their counterparts in high tension communities. A similar but weaker trend is apparent for noncollege respondents.

TABLE 7

COMMUNITY CLIMATE IN RELATION TO READING
OF THE KERNER REPORT

	College Respondent		Noncollege Respondent	
	High Tension Community	Low Tension Community	High Tension Community	Low Tension Community
Reading the Kerner Report	28.3%	32.9%	11.0%	N.S. 13.2%
Not Reading the Kerner Report	71.7	67.1	89.0	86.8
	100.0%	100.0%	100.0%	100.0%
	(N=180)	(N=134)	(N=262)	(169)

In Table 8 the extent of tension expressed by Kerner Report readers is compared for college and noncollege respondents. For the former group no community climate effects appear to be present. Moreover readers and non-readers within the college group show no differences in perceptions of riot anxiety by peers. A sharply different picture is present for the noncollege respondents. Here, being in a high tension community means nearly three times as many readers of the Kerner Report see their peers as "very concerned" about a future riot. Community climate has a slight effect in the same direction for nonreaders in the same educational cluster.

Educational level is an important predictor of how the Kerner Report is perceived. Thus for both readers and nonreaders of the report 28.6% of the college respondents see the major finding to be racism; 14.4% of the noncollege respondents pick this interpretation. By contrast 24.8% of noncollege respondents pick the conclusion that militants caused the riots; only 12.2% of the college respondents select this interpretation. This suggests one important difference occurs within the white suburban community: that between the college and noncollege family.

To examine the role of community climate on education groupings Table 9 presents data on the racism and militant theses. The question we are posing is this: Given the proclivities of interpretation for the college and noncollege group, how is this altered by the riot climate of the community in which the reader resides? The findings indicated by Table 9 show important "contextual" effects. Thus, for the racism thesis, college readers of the Kerner Report are significantly less likely to pick the "correct" interpretation where they live in a high riot tension community. At the same time,

TABLE 11

INFLUENCE OF COMMUNITY CLIMATE: SUPPORT AND
OPPOSITION TO CHANGING INSTITUTIONAL PATTERNS:
HIGH VERSUS LOW RIOT TENSION SUBURBS

	High Riot Tension			Low Riot Tension			
	Support	Oppose		Support	Oppose		
neighborhood ~gration in your ~munity	40%	50%	−10%	55%	35%	+20%	SIGN.
~ organize a ~ram to evaluate ~m in your police ~rtment	48	39	+ 9	41	42	− 1	N.S.
~ organize a pro-~ to evaluate racism ~e school system	52	36	+16	52	34	+18	N.S.
~nize a group of ~e to go into ~ ghettoes to ~as needed	48	41	+ 7	47	40	+ 7	N.S.
~financial support ~ups seeking Negro ~ol over Negro ~borhoods	27	63	−36	26	58	−32	N.S.
~e your present ~unity if you ~ it was not going ~ange its racial ~ns	15	71	−56	16	69	−53	N.S.
	(N=469)			(N=319)			

The findings which we have presented suggest several processes which ~ account for the relationships demonstrated. One theory argues that ~bs are vast sifting and sorting units in which the white middle-class ~n chooses a community that fits his values and life goals. Another the-~gues for the changes which a person undergoes once they come into the ~ world of a given community. Let us label the first explanation the ~tion model"—people are going to fit into a community which will only ~rce their preexisting values. The second explanation we can call the

---

TABLE 8

COMMUNITY CLIMATE IN RELATION TO CONCERN
ABOUT NEW RACIAL DISORDERS
FOR BLUE- AND WHITE-COLLAR FAMILIES

"Considering the neighbors and the people you know, how concerned would you say they are about the likelihood of new racial disorders in the coming months (summer 1968)?"

	College Respondents			Noncollege Respondents		
	High Tension Community		Low Tension Community	High Tension Community		Low Tension Community
Read the Kerner Report	49.0%* (N=51)	N.S.	52.3% (N=44)	62.0% (N=29)	SIGN.	22.7% (N=22)
Not Read the Kerner Report	48.0% (N=129)	N.S.	53.3% (N=90)	45.5% (N=233)	N.S.	42.9% (N=147)

*Percentages are based on question responses of "very concerned." Other possible responses are "somewhat concerned," "not very concerned," "not at all concerned," and "don't know."

TABLE 9

COMMUNITY CLIMATE IN RELATION TO PERCEIVED
FINDINGS OF THE KERNER REPORT

	College Respondents			Noncollege Respondents		
	High Tension Community		Low Tension Community	High Tension Community		Low Tension Community
"Whites have Created a Built-in Racist System"	31.9%		43.5%	27.6%		18.2%
Read Report		SIGN.			SIGN.	
"Militant Groups Caused the Riots"	6.4		19.4	38.0		13.7
Read Report		SIGN.			SIGN.	
	(N=51)		(N=44)	(N=29)		(N=22)

the noncollege reader living in the high tension setting picks the incorrect militant thesis three times as often as in a low tension community. Ironically noncollege readers in a high tension community also select the racism thesis more often than when they reside in a low tension community. Moreover, Table 9 shows that the militant thesis is chosen three times as often by college readers of the Kerner Report when they reside in a low tension community.

To summarize, we find that community climate importantly affects how readers of the Kerner Report interpret its meaning. College readers choose both the racism and militant thesis in a low tension community. Noncollege readers display this pattern in high tension communities. Clearly, then, an interaction effect occurs between the role of community climate and the educational level of respondents.

Additional Community Context Effects

To further specify the interaction between educational groupings and community climate Table 10 presents data on the five components of the riot tension index. College-educated respondents are significantly lower in perceptions about neighbor and friend riot reactions in low tension communities. Noncollege respondents show significant climate differentials for 2 of the 5 indices. These findings reflect the role of community context regardless of the educational level of the respondent.

Our discussion of the role of community climate has indicated the significance of this variable for riot perceptions and attitudes. The question of the ultimate effects of such a factor was analyzed in two ways: reactions to a set of proposals to ease race tensions and subsequent voting in the presidential election of November 1968.

Table 11 contains data on how persons of different socioeconomic levels were affected by community climate in evaluating courses of action to alleviate race tensions. The question was asked: "How much would you support each of these ideas?" Community climate significantly affected responses to only one of the six proposals—aiding neighborhood integration. In low tension communities 20% more favored this action than opposed it; in high tension communities 10% more opposed it than favored it. A similar direction but not statistically significant is found for the suggested evaluation of police racism.

In Table 12 the question of aiding integration is used to further pinpoint the effects of climate. Socioeconomic groupings are shown and the effects of climate within the specified categories. In all comparisons we find

TABLE 10

COMMUNITY CLIMATE IN RELATION TO BLUE-COL
AND WHITE-COLLAR PERCEPTIONS OF TENSION

	College Respondents			Noncollege
	High Tension Community	Low Tension Community		High Tension Community
Contacting Police about Riot Dangers	33%*	25%	SIGN.	31%
Reading Pamphlets about Riot Dangers	48	39	SIGN.	41
Attending Meetings about Riot Dangers	37	34	N.S.	28
Purchasing Firearms to Protect Against Riot Dangers	63	59	N.S.	56
Taking Training in the use of Firearms	31	19	SIGN.	29
	(N=180)	(N=134)		(N=262

*Percent of respondents indicating that "a few," "some," or "ma
and friends" have been active in doing the indicated behavior.

that socioeconomic level predicts significantly how int
Note that white- versus blue-collar respondents show a –
—24% figure—a differential of 29%. But this is match
differences between high and low riot tension commu
nounced differences occur when education is used as t
Income shows similar but somewhat muted differences.

Our final analysis deals with voting behavior. He
measures but only community voting patterns obtained
following the elections of November 1968. Table 13
data. Our focus is the Wallace vote. Communities hi
"barometer" are also highest on the level of Wallace v
rank-order correlation for the nine communities is +.
the nine communities in the study had a Wallace voting
national total of 9.8% of the votes cast.

TABLE 12

COMMUNITY CLIMATE: EFFECTS ON DIFFERENT SOCIOECONOMIC GROUPS
IN RELATION TO REDUCING RACE TENSION THROUGH INTEGRATION

		Aid Neighborhood Integration		
		High	Low	
Occupation:				
	White-Collar	+ 5%*	+34%	SIGN.
	Blue-Collar	−24%	+ 5%	SIGN.
Education:				
	College	+ 2%	+34%	SIGN.
	Noncollege	−20%	+ 9%	SIGN.
Income:				
	10,000 or more	− 7%	+26%	SIGN.
	under 10,000	− 8%	+13%	SIGN.

*Percentages represent the difference between supporting and opposing responses to each item. Thus a "+" percentage denotes more support than opposition; a "−" means more opposition than support.

TABLE 13

VOTING PATTERNS OF SATELLITE COMMUNITIES
IN NOVEMBER 1968 PRESIDENTIAL ELECTION:
TOTAL WALLACE VOTE*

	Total Vote	Percent of Wallace Vote Among Registered Voters
Warren (H)	9,444	15.7
Southgate (H)	1,717	15.2
Madison Heights (L)	1,841	14.8
East Detroit (H)	2,532	13.1
Dearborn (H)	6,292	11.6
Livonia (L)	4,025	10.0
Plymouth (L)	411	8.6
Royal Oak (L)	3,074	8.0
Southfield (H)	1,543	5.4
Average		11.4%

*The statistics in this table are based on personal communication of the research staff with city clerks in the various communities as of November 28, 1968.

"socialization model"—people are affected by the social interaction they have with friends and neighbors in their community setting.

In Table 14 some evaluation of the role of each theory of community climate is provided. The data are presented in terms of "newcomers" and "old-timers" to each of the nine communities. If the "selection model" were to be supported we would have to find in Table 14 evidence that newcomers as well as old-timers share general similar orientations. Were the "socialization model" to be upheld we should find newcomers to be different from old-timers. Examining Table 14, the data give rather firm support to a socialization process—newcomers come to share the values of those already in a community. There is another possible explanation of these same findings: Persons who differ from the community may decide to leave as quickly as they can to find a more compatible setting. While this may, in fact, occur it is clear that many families cannot generally act on such issues since a household move is one of the most important decisions a young family has to make. Moreover, we cannot assume that people are actually conscious of the value-molding influences of a community. This is not a formal process. It occurs in a subtle fashion and is the product of all the stimuli coming to a person from contacts within his community.

TABLE 14

REACTIONS TO SIX STEPS TO CHANGE RACE RELATIONS FOR "NEWCOMERS" AND "OLD-TIMERS" IN COMMUNITIES

	Living in Community 2 Years or Less	Living in Community over 2 Years
Aid neighborhood integration	+19%	− 5%
Evaluate racism in schools	+38	+16
Go into the ghetto to help	+20	+ 8
Evaluate police racism	+17	± 0
Finance self-determination	−44	−24
Leave your community if it was not going to change	−40	−55
	(N=130)	(N=652)

*Percentages refer to differences between support or opposition to the suggested program. A "+" means more support than opposition.

In terms of the data shown in Table 14 we have found further support for the role of community climate. Newcomers appear to undergo change in conformity with the values of their neighbors. This may be a process which supports social change or retards it. The outcome depends on the climate of that particular community.

Conclusions and Implications

Although our findings are not always consistent, we have illustrated the role of riot tension as a force which cuts across groups within a community and provides a collective response to race issues. This further underlines the fact that suburbanites live not merely in a world isolated from the black community but also within an atmosphere characteristic of a second-order isolation—the climate of an individual suburb.

The results of the current study offer more of a framework for analysis than a link to specific ways to alter race relations. However, the following considerations seem to warrant further attention in light of our findings.

1. *A high degree of informational distortion characterizes the white suburbanite's knowledge of black community priorities.* The role of the mass media in creating a basis for judging events of the inner city is substantial. One of the great paradoxes of the mass media is that during periods of crisis or great change, it is most difficult for the rather impersonal and oversimplified messages of the media to change attitudes and reach an audience that has already been affected by "pictures" rather than words. This means that efforts to change attitudes of white suburbanites are only able to succeed where daily events can be utilized as a foundation on which to build new attitudes. Given the "crisis" definition by both liberal and racist groups, neither exhortation nor threat can influence those who have "tuned-out" the message and see only what they want to see. Certainly, the distortion of Kerner Report findings reflects more of the mass media's coverage than actual reading of the analysis. Media efforts must define a target population that is "listening" and can then go out to talk face-to-face with neighbors and friends who are "not listening."

2. *Programs of community change must be geared to the socioeconomic characteristics of suburbs.* Wide differences in population composition exist and reflect different forms of racism, race tension, and support for given changes. By differentiating goals in terms of "where people are," a more effective impact can be anticipated. Suburbs are far from identical. To stereotype them is just as dangerous as stereotyping the residents of the central city. Part of this effort must be to avoid bases of conflict that might undermine constructive programs. Thus, if white-collar suburbs are more preoccupied with social class issues, it is better to utilize this for specific actions and not tie these in with efforts in blue-collar communities where hostility is more evident but based more narrowly on race conflict. The opportunity for

coalition between blue-collar communities and black community residents has a basis for providing a common "class" front once the race focus is put in context. Thus both blue-collar suburbanites and black inner-city residents face many common problems of the "system" treating them as an "underclass."

3. *Suburban communities create their own isolated worlds and are not in the minds of its residents satellites of the central city.* There is a great need to make suburbanites aware that the parochialism of their community hides the interdependence of their fate with that of the black inner city. This relationship of mutual interaction is not understood by most suburbanites. Educational efforts to point out institutional linkages to the city and to racial minorities is a first-priority educational task.

4. *Finally, groups and individuals interested in social change in the suburbs must recognize the need to build "indigenous" leadership.* In the same manner that the poverty programs of the inner city have sought to build a basis for participation and decision making, so must this occur in the suburbs. Suburbs are not going to be changed by outsiders. In fact, such groups are analogous to the paternalistic whites who have tended to control Negro civil rights efforts: Change to be valid must be built from within. This means, first of all, that moderate groups in the suburbs must be brought into the process of change rather than polarizing communities through highly visible ideological tactics.

The tremendous force for change represented by the alienated youth of suburbia must be tapped as a potentially significant resource. Frequently, the sons and daughters of upper-middle-class families go to far-off campuses to protest war, racism, and student subjugation. They do not focus their energies on their own communities. If this process of youthful commitment and change focused on the local community could be developed, perhaps a series of interlinked problems of suburbia can be ameliorated.

5. *It is important to take the struggle for racial justice out of an ideological context.* Suburbanites are going to respond to programs of change that are self-serving and pragmatic. It is the task of all groups interested in solving race problems and bringing the suburbs back into society to recognize the realities of community climate and then seek to redirect them.

Appendix

TABLE A

POPULATION AND GROWTH RATE OF THE DETROIT
SUBURBAN COMMUNITIES

Community	Population 4/1/60	Population 7/1/67	Change #	%
Warren	89,246	173,500	84,254	94
Dearborn	112,007	115,000	2,993	3
Livonia	66,702	101,000	34,298	51
Royal Oak	80,612	96,000	15,388	19
Southfield	31,531	65,000	33,469	106
East Detroit	45,756	47,000	1,244	3
Madison Heights	33,343	38,200	4,857	15
Southgate	29,404	33,700	4,296	15
Plymouth	8,766	11,500	2,734	31
Total	497,367	680,900	183,533	337

Source: *Southeastern Michigan Council of Governments,* March 1968.

TABLE B

CHARACTERISTICS OF SURVEY SAMPLE FOR THE NINE SUBURBS
(Communities ordered by occupational level)

	Percent Income of $10,000 or More	Percent More Than High School Education	Percent White-Collar Occupations	
Southfield	76.1 (73.1)*	55.9 (46.7)	66.4 (72.7)	White-Collar
Livonia	72.5 (52.2)	51.2 (44.7)	60.7 (60.6)	
Royal Oak	55.0 (39.7)	46.9 (40.5)	60.2 (60.5)	
Plymouth	51.7 (46.6)	36.5 (40.8)	50.8 (55.8)	
Dearborn	47.6 (33.5)	39.7 (32.3)	50.7 (55.5)	
Warren	60.0 (32.8)	34.6 (24.7)	45.4 (39.5)	Blue-Collar
Madison Heights	41.5 (23.5)	31.0 (24.1)	39.5 (38.7)	
Southgate	48.1 (33.8)	32.8 (17.0)	36.1 (29.4)	
East Detroit	32.1 (35.7)	24.2 (18.7)	33.9 (36.2)	

*Percentages in parentheses are the Traffic and Land Use Study (TALUS) figures for 1965-66.

TABLE C

QUESTIONNAIRE RESPONSE RATE FOR THE NINE
SUBURBAN COMMUNITIES: JUNE 1968

	Base	Percent Completing Questionnaire[a]	Percent Contacted[b]	Percent Not Contacted[c]
Livonia	100	84.0	95.0	5.0
Southfield	100	77.0	92.0	8.0
Madison Heights	100	71.0	89.0	11.0
Dearborn	200	68.0	90.1	9.9
Royal Oak	150	65.3	88.6	11.4
Warren	200	65.0	89.0	11.0
Plymouth	100	63.0	88.0	12.0
East Detroit	100	62.0	91.0	9.0
Southgate	100	61.0	87.0	13.0
Totals	1150	68.8	90.2	9.8

a. Returned questionnaire by mail or interviewed on telephone.
b. Includes refusals or return of blank questionnaire.
c. Includes persons without correct telephone number or not residing at given address, or no contact obtained.

TABLE D

Selected Riot Causes as Perceived by Detroit Area Negroes and Whites
—Rank Ordered—

Negro Respondents in Detroit			White Detroiters		
Riot Area Negroes (August 1967)[a]	Northwest Detroit (December 1967)[b]	Detroit Middle-Income Survey (May 1968)[c]	Northwest Detroit (December 1967)[d]	Detroit Middle-Income Survey (May 1968)[e]	Satellite Suburbs (June 1968)[f]
Police brutality	Poor housing	Police brutality	Black nationalism	Teen-agers	Black nationalism
Poor housing	Lack of jobs	Poor housing	Poverty	Black nationalism	Poverty
Lack of jobs	Poverty	Lack of jobs	Poor housing	Too much welfare	Lack of jobs
Poverty	Police brutality	Poverty	Lack of jobs	Poor housing	Poor housing
Disappointment with white public officials	Disappointment with white public officials	Disappointment with white public officials	Teen-agers	Poverty	Too much welfare
Teen-agers	Teen-agers	Teen-agers	Too much welfare	Lack of jobs	Teen-agers
Black nationalism	Black nationalism	Black nationalism	Disappointment with white public officials	Disappointment with white public officials	Disappointment with white public officials
——*	Too much welfare	Too much welfare	Police brutality	Police brutality	Police brutality

[a] 437 respondents
[b] 188 respondents
[c] 392 respondents
[d] 213 respondents
[e] 208 respondents
[f] 788 respondents
* "Too much welfare" not listed in this survey.

Community Consensus as a Goal Seeking Constructive Change*

Donald Lief

In the year after the awesome destruction of last July's riots, all that can safely be said is that Detroit will never be the same. Whether the change will be good enough cannot yet be answered. Meanwhile, leadership of the nation's fifth-largest city speaks a new language and operates with new rules. Lying amidst the uncleared rubble and burned-out buildings are the broken clichés of how to make a model community.

Detroit's traditional business power structure has been realigned; sweeping changes in the city government have been proposed; Negro groups are more organized, more articulate than before. The city is by no means a house undivided. Right-wing groups urge whites to arm themselves in expectation of further racial violence. Black radicals don't rule out a decade of guerrilla warfare. Thus, the quest for rapid progress takes place in a fluid, extremely risky situation.

The urgent need for action is the constant theme reiterated by three diverse leaders: Mayor Jerome P. Cavanagh, department store executive Joseph L. Hudson, Jr., and Rev. Albert B. Cleage, Jr., spiritual leader and chief ideologue of Detroit's black nationalist movement.

All three can show some institutional results: Mayor Cavanagh on August 3 named two of his former top aides as heads of a Mayor's Development Team with the mission of "creating a blueprint for the social and physical development of the city." Working under crash deadlines, the team produced a monumental 750-page report which the mayor presented October 26, 84 days later. To some extent an agonizing reappraisal of municipal agencies' performance, the study proposed that many activities be central-

From: "Detroit Seeks to Bring Constructive Change Out of the Summer's Chaos," in *City*, bi-monthly review of Urban America, January 1968, Volume 2, Number 1, pp. 5-8. Reprinted with permission.
*EDITOR'S NOTE: This article contains some information on the New Detroit Committee that appears in the article earlier in part three from the *Detroit Scope* magazine. However, the perspective here focuses primarily on attempts at accommodation rather than community conflicts and communication breakdowns.

ized within two new superagencies, one for social development, the other for physical development, as well as redirection of other departments.

Coalition

Shortly after the riots, Cavanagh joined with Gov. George Romney in asking Hudson to form a New Detroit Committee to muster the community's major private resources. Businessman Hudson chose 39 of the city's most influential business and labor leaders along with some of the more outspokenly hostile Negro militants. Quickly known as "the Hudson committee," the group's members include: Henry Ford II; Lynn Townsend, chairman of Chrysler Corp.; James Roche, president of General Motors Corp.; two local university presidents; the city school superintendent; the majority leader of the state senate; the minority leader of the state house, and Walter P. Reuther, president of the United Auto Workers. Also included were Norvel Harrington, an 18-year-old Negro student who helped organize the citywide Black Power group; Alvin Harrison, president of the militant Afro-American Unity movement; Mrs. Lena Bivens, a well-regarded neighborhood leader; and Lorenzo Freeman, director of a Saul Alinsky-spawned neighborhood West Side Organization.

The committee was staffed through loans of manpower from the members; a utilities firm provided space and office equipment. The staff was made available for an initial 90 days. In mid-December, Hudson said he had received "a brand new open line from contributors of staff for the same people or others of comparable quality for the next five months." Several bank vice presidents, heads of economics, research, and engineering departments, and other specialists give the committee staff strong competence.

What has such leadership achieved? Joseph Hudson said, "We have created a meaningful dialogue . . . we have mobilized a greater sense of urgency on jobs, we have added a greater sense of conscience on fair housing." The New Detroit Committee lobbied the special session of the Michigan legislature for several key measures. It lost the first test, a $5.3-million fund for mobile classrooms in the city. Then at Christmas time, the state legislation will be introduced to require any insurance firm doing business in Michigan to provide some basic fire and property coverage in slums. A pool concept, jointly developed by the Hudson Committee and the state insurance commissioner, already had shown impact; it was feared that many policies would be cancelled automatically 90 days after the riots, but many companies extended their coverage. In anticipation of the bill, further extensions are expected.

Under the aegis of the Hudson Committee, a "Homes by Christmas" drive produced $180,000 in contributions from the entire community to provide a revolving loan fund for housing. Some 120 ghetto families made homeless by the riots were the first beneficiaries. By early 1968, they will be buying their own homes, thanks to $1500 loans—$1,000 for down payment and $500 for basic necessities. Most had been renting; they were not public housing or welfare families, but they had thought they would always be renters. Metropolitan Life Insurance pledged mortgage money if the dwellings were approved by FHA.

Actions by the New Detroit Committee to gain more jobs for inner-city residents resulted in some 33,000 new jobs created since August, involving 76 companies. Impressive as the number is, even more striking was the hiring approach of some employers. Ford Motor Co. changed some of its standards and began to recruit in poor neighborhoods. "If they want jobs, we'll give them jobs," Henry Ford II told the *New York Times.* "And we are not going to give them tests." Rather than weighing competence for a particular job, Ford began to test "cultural background." A lengthy orientation period was also part of the new Ford hiring approach.

In the sensitive area of police and law enforcement, the committee commissioned a top-to-bottom study of the Detroit police department from Michigan State University. The study, however, will take three years.

Self-Determination

In addition to its own activities, the New Detroit Committee soon made it clear that it would work with Negro organizations, whether moderate or militant, separatist or integrationist. The ensuing triangular relationship between the Hudson Committee, the Black Power groups, and the old-line Negro leadership developed carefully, cautiously during the summer and fall. But by January, mistrust and misunderstanding had cracked, if not shattered, these fragile relationships.

The key figure was Rev. Cleage, whose Central United Church of Christ attracts both militants and moderates to services. The 56-year-old pastor, increasingly regarded as the ideological spokesman for the majority of Detroit's Negroes, moved quickly after the riots to start the Citywide Citizens' Action Committee (CCAC), possibly the most broadly based Black Power organization in any city. Cleage declared, "This movement has self-determination, and black control of the black community is our purpose."

CCAC paralleled the structure of the New Detroit Committee: Each set up working groups to deal with communications, public and private community services, education, employment, law, finances, and redevelopment. In addition, CCAC deals with ministerial relations, political organization and voter registration, civil service, and culture.

Cooperative action received heavy emphasis: CCAC's Black Star Co-Op Inc. opened its first grocery store in December; others are planned as well as light industry.

In housing, CCAC will emphasize rehabilitation on a cooperative basis and construction of low-income dwellings. With $100,000 reportedly received from church denominations, CCAC will hire black professionals and technicians to help plan restoration of the inner city.

Separatist as he is, Cleage said of CCAC, "Our main holdup is getting lending funds for small business development. We have found some white, private investors who are interested in our cooperatives. They are willing to let us use their money but allow us to direct the course of our business. We have not found resistance to our plans in either the white or black community."

Along with CCAC's programs, Cleage assembled an impressive brain trust of young professionals, all committed to black self-determination.

Reaction to the CCAC was violent among the moderate, largely middle-class Detroit Council of Organizations which includes rival ministers, union officials (mostly United Auto Workers), and Democratic party functionaries. The DCO issued its "Local Action Program for a New Detroit"—with calls for open housing, better land use, improved schools, and jobs.

Possibly to minimize friction, Cleage moved to a broader position in December by creating The Federation for Self-Determination, a non-partisan, non-sectarian, and non-profit umbrella covering moderate as well as militant views and groups. As its first steps, The Federation is acting as a forum, a catalyst for cooperation and programs, and a research center. It also plans to provide technical assistance to slum groups.

In December, Cleage announced that the organization would seek Hudson Committee support. Joseph Hudson and his committee endorsed the concept of an inner-city federation as "absolutely not inconsistent with the American dream" and encouraged The Federation to broaden its membership so the request for funds could be seriously considered.

With the New Detroit Committee's links to the militants visibly closer, the DCO responded by charging the committee with failure to deal with "responsible Negroes." And, in turn, it submitted a proposal to start its own program for the slums.

At its January 4 meeting, the New Detroit Committee, faced with the two competing groups and programs, sought to assist each by offering two $100,000 grants on a 50-50 matching basis. That evening, The Federation convened in Cleage's church and unanimously rejected the money. Cleage denounced the conditions: (1) a prohibition on partisan activity to conform with Internal Revenue rules, (2) opportunity for other groups to participate, (3) regular auditing, and (4) a committee liaison man. He charged, "Whites have tried to absorb blacks paternalistically and then on terms set by whites." Committee members Harrington and Freeman resigned; "We were on the committee only as show pieces."

By refusing "whitey's money," Cleage's stock soared among Negroes. He said other funds would finance The Federation. Hudson, meanwhile, dismayed at events, attributed them to misunderstanding and sought "to keep lines of communication open."

Involvement or Control

Throughout the turmoil of the winter, Mayor Cavanagh's administration has been preoccupied with the massive MDT report. It was not applauded by the militants. Cleage called it "shallow because it leans heavily on police suppression of the black community." He said it contains "all the reports the city has put together for the past 10 years, only this time they are under one cover." Dr. Karl D. Gregory, a Wayne State University economics professor and adviser to CCAC, said, "It was a quickie effort to appear impressive." There is some agreement among the white leadership. Said one influential businessman: "The MDT report lacks thrust, and it's questionable whether a 90-day report under such stress can do the job."

Richard Strichartz, former city controller, now general counsel of Wayne State University, who served as coordinator of the report, defended it. The report, he said, would not be acceptable to black militants—regardless of contents—"unless they wrote it, and then it would not represent the thinking of all Negroes." While community relations are emphasized in recommendations dealing with the police department, he said, "Community participation is a thread throughout the whole thing."

Clearly the matter of citizen involvement and citizen control is touchy. Strichartz made the distinction: Citizen involvement is everything short of actions which would require legal authority. If Detroit wants to confer greater control of governmental programs and services upon its neighborhood residents, implied Strichartz, "they have the ballot box." But the MDT report, while it blazes no new trails in political theory, establishes some important goals for the city's departments.

Far from a placid document, it rips into many aspects of the city. There are too many different job training programs so that "the efficacy is problematical." Parks and Recreation was termed "an ingrown agency" that is "viewed with hostility" by a large segment of the city.

The tough approach of the MDT report raised some bureaucratic hackles and, doubtless, will face stiff resistance also from the Common Council when and if some of the proposals are in the form of charter revisions.

Mayor Cavanagh, however, plunged into implementation of the report with characteristic energy. One source close to City Hall said, "Cavanagh has demonstrated more leadership since July than ever before, even at the height of his popularity." The mayor's position is that the riots exposed the deficiencies of the existing programs, that the city knows now what it should be doing.

Pushing his department heads, Cavanagh asked for detailed reactions to the MDT study, with their short-term and long-term priorities. Then he required biweekly progress reports. His own staff took on the task of overseeing implementation of the MDT.

Strichartz saw police-community relations as one of the most obvious fields where the city government could act swiftly to show progress. Following up, the city administration took a number of steps: By early January, it opened three store-front neighborhood communications units manned by police seven days a week. The police are empowered to act as virtual ombudsmen in ferreting out answers to citizen complaints, not only about police actions but also about housing code enforcement or any other municipal service. James T. Trainor, secretary of the mayor's MDT subcommittee, admits that these units cannot investigate as thoroughly as would an ombudsman, but "if they have any trouble in responding from a city agency, they're to call me." Meanwhile, the city's departments and bureaus have been informed that they must do more than merely noting complaints.

To further community relations, the police department now requires its inspectors to walk a portion of a beat each day—alone. Some point out they have been doing it since the summer anyway. Going beyond this, inspectors will now work an occasional night shift and in their cruisers, not behind desks, in order to respond to calls. Only two of 23 inspectors, and 3.4 per cent of the force, are Negro. But the police have greatly intensified their efforts at Negro recruitment.

In the field of development, Mayor Cavanagh took a major step by funding the salary of an advocate planner for the Virginia Park rehabilitation of riot-gutted 12 Street. The neighborhood grass-roots organization will be able to hire and fire its own planner. This is reportedly the first instance of a municipality's paying for this degree of resident involvement.

MDT coordinator Strichartz emphasized that, despite the length and sprawling nature of his report, there is a common denominator to all its recommendations: "There is a climate now for listening and responding to citizens; responding is more important than listening."

The difficulty of achieving substantial program changes rapidly in Detroit seems enormous when measured against the magnitude of change required. So the various leadership efforts may be one day viewed as empty exercises, which failed to ward off catastrophe. But, somehow, one gains the impression that Detroit's institutions, municipal, civic, and neighborhood, are continually goaded by the turning pages of the calendar. It is this awareness which may determine what Detroit will be like in the future.

The Crisis in Our Cities
An Action Perspective

Mel Ravitz

No analysis of our cities and their problems can succeed without first defining and describing what the city is and what it is becoming.

In his masterful book, *The Culture of Cities,* Lewis Mumford defined "the city in its complete sense" as:

". . . a geographic plexus, an economic organization, an institutional process, a theater of social action, and an aesthetic symbol of collective unity."

In other words, the city is a thing of many dimensions: a site, a social system and setting, and a symbol.

The city is one other thing: It is the product of the technology, the social relationships and the ideas of a people. This means that the city reflects the cultural forces that have shaped it for good or ill over the years. As a reflection of the culture of the larger society, the problems of the city are those of the whole society. Although ultimately the crisis of our cities will be met only when we have confronted the basic issues of the larger society and satisfactorily resolved them, it is true that the arena in which to confront these issues is the city.

Accordingly, it is necessary to examine some of the problems of today's cities, and to consider what is required to resolve them.

A fundamental fact of our national life is that our cities continue to grow in land area and to increase in population. For example, the more than four million people of the Detroit region will become five million by 1975, and will be seven million by the year two thousand. We are expanding northeasterly towards Port Huron and southerly towards Toledo. Long ago we outgrew the concept of the city. We have become the megalopolis or the metroplex, whichever you prefer.

The author is a member of the Wayne State University Sociology Department and a Detroit Councilman. This article is previously unpublished.

Historically the move has been towards larger and larger human clusters. Size and population have been based on the available water and food supplies. Now however, modern technology has minimized the importance of these factors. One wonders how large we should permit our urban concentrations to grow, which question presupposes we possess the skill to control their size and population if we wished.

The crisis of our cities and of our society arises from a complex of gigantic problems, which may be summarized rather simply but which as yet defy solution.

One present and emerging problem concerns facilities. The sheer population growth and spread, together with a rising expectation of improved quality, demands immense quantities of houses, schools, hospitals, libraries, stores, factories, roads, water, drainage and sewage systems, recreation sites, churches, etc. We are embarked upon an era of unbelievable competition for land for these multiple and often incompatible uses. Questions we shall have to answer are these: How can we best utilize the available land to meet the needs of our swelling population? What shall be the relationship of the individual's right to land as against the community's needs? How will we pay for these additional facilities, especially the public ones? What combination of local, state, federal and private funds is the right one?

Another problem of related concern is pollution of air, water, and land. As the value of land increases, we must be vitally concerned not only with its wise use and reuse, but also with eliminating such inferior and immoral land uses as slums. We have begun to discover that an integral element of urban renewal and other displacement projects is human relocation. To date we have virtually ignored this consequence of clearance. We have uprooted people from their homes and shifted and shunted them around the community without compassion. We have not provided sufficient compensation to make people whole again, or to upgrade their housing from the slums we destroyed. We have not communicated effectively with those we are displacing to assure them that we care about them and view them as civilian casualties of the war to renew our cities. We have not yet built the low and medium cost housing of varied sizes and costs and styles to meet the shelter needs of those we displace as well as the needs of countless others who simply seek to improve their housing circumstances. In all these things we have failed, and people have begun to wonder if their slums are not better than the arrogance and inhumanity of urban renewal.

Another pollution problem concerns disposal of our solid wastes and garbage. No longer can this problem be handled efficiently on a separate municipality basis. We shall have to solve this problem on a broad regional basis, or it will not be solved at all. Likewise with urban air and water pollution, which, happily, we have now at least placed on our agenda.

The cost of meeting these several pollution problems is high. Yet, failure to do so means the risk of self-destruction from being buried in our own debris, or from being smothered in putrid air, or from foul water sources. No aspect of the crisis of our cities is more imminent than the pollution of our environment. We have now reached the stage of where we must conserve and renew our land, water, and air, not just for the sake of natural beauty or for future generations, but for our own contemporary survival.

As more and more people have crowded into our cities, significant population shifts have been occurring. Today we can discern more distinct lines of segregation than ever before. The old, inner core area of the central city, which traditionally has been heavily black and poor, is now being bulldozed piecemeal and being rebuilt with freeway links, luxury housing, civic centers, and specialized area for business, health care, and education. Middle- and upper-class whites and some blacks are replacing the former predominantly black population. We are participating in, as well as witnessing, an ecological revolution, as the inside of the city is being pushed out into the next ring of neighborhoods.

New slums are now being nurtured in these adjacent neighborhoods, as poor people are permitted to overcrowd and overuse the housing units, and as landlords exploit their properties through zoning· variances, ineffective code enforcement, and minimal maintenance.

Meanwhile, in the fringes and the suburbs of the metroplex, the majority of white middle-class citizens live in their ranch type, colonial, split level or development structures, essentially oblivious of the rest of mankind, particularly those who are black, who are poor, who are old, who are unskilled, uneducated, and sometimes unemployed.

It required the riot of July 23, 1967, to attract some brief attention to the inner city and its complex problems of our making. And that riot with its violence and destruction both deepened the fears of many white people, even as it raised the level of militancy of many blacks. Cultivation of these fears concurrent with the rise of this militancy is a combination calculated to encourage future violence.

It is clear that Detroit and other urban centers are in a desperate race with time. Can we build improved relationships between white and black people, between the well-to-do and the poor, between inner city residents and suburbanites? Can we unify our region while respecting the legitimate interests and rights of black people who want their share of autonomy and power? Can we muster the sense of urgency as well as the intelligent actions necessary to create a livable community before another catastrophe explodes?

Not only do we face a direct and continuing bitter confrontation between black and white in the area of the urban community, but we also face an almost certain conflict between the disadvantaged of both races, on the one hand, and on the other hand those who are reasonably well off, and who today never had it so good, even after taxes. The city is the scene to which the Negro revolution has shifted and where it must be won. And this revolution to win full civil rights for all Americans is intimately tied to the economic revolution, which is just getting underway.

The main thrust of the civil rights movement is to permit black people to live, to learn, to work, to play, to grow, and to participate in all phases of community life in the same way as everyone else. And to do so peacefully, with dignity and now. One of the participants in the Watts riot of 1965 is reported to have put the matter more bluntly:

What this is all about is the gravy of this great society. We want some of it, brother . . . yeah, and a piece of the steak. We want in.

And what the black person wants, the poor white wants too, only he has been less articulate and organized about expressing it.

Although the problems of race and poverty are separate, they are interrelated. The black and white poor want jobs; job training; merit employment and upgrading; sound, suitable, and sufficient housing at prices they can afford; quality education for their children; effective law enforcement. And they want this within the context of increasing automation and cybernation. Both unskilled blacks and whites question whether they will be able to maintain jobs in the face of efficiency and the economy of the machine. They wonder who will work in the days ahead when machines assume more and more of the work of men and women. They are curious whether there will be a work elite which alone will be privileged to apply its talents to production and service. They are concerned about the fate of those who do not work. They are anxious about their social status in a society dominated by technology and demanding only the highest human auxiliary skills.

Although I cannot of course allay these fears which relate to a new definition of work, I do know they will not be resolved by the tool of the so-called war on poverty. That war as we see it waged in the cities across the country is really just a skirmish, a well-intentioned flourish without appropriate priorities, without objective evaluation, and without very much substance.

Still another part of the crisis of the city is the problem of social deviancy. This problem assumes several forms. Deviancy is evident in the growing number of violent crimes committed by adults and youth in our cities. It is evident in the overall lawlessness of so many white-collar folks who break the law quietly by deceit, collusion, connivery. Deviancy is evident in the incidence of mental and emotional illness we are now beginning to acknowledge and treat. It is evident too in the shifting moral code we sometimes emphasize, sometimes elude, sometimes wink at. In one way or another our society and its urban focal points find more and more of their members deviating from the rest of us.

Ancient moral standards no longer seem to apply. But we have not yet developed firm new standards. Today's urban society is massive, impersonal, mobile; people move within it anonymously. They come and go as passing shadows, and few of us can tell who does what. What is worse, we seem utterly uninterested in what happens to anyone else. Our motto has become: "Don't get involved."

Cardinal questions confronting the city and the society are—How do we develop and teach a new, viable moral code for everyday behavior? How do we discourage crime and delinquency of both the violent sort and the white-collar kind? How do we establish and affirm a clear purpose for participation in the community? How do we help ourselves adapt to the unbelievable social and psychological pressures of modern life without the special services of the psychiatrist or the mental hospitals?

These then are just some of the salient problems that constitute the crisis of our cities. Space does not permit review of such other acute problems as education, transportation, regional administration. With all our urban problems the old adage applies: We shape our cities and our cities shape us. Every day of failure to resolve these immense problems further confounds them and consigns countless people to lives of wretchedness, fear, and despair. Yet there is no simple solution. At best, community organizational meetings may spark a clue or two to help us move in the right direction. At worst, such meetings pamper the middle-class myth that if well-intentioned people talk about something long enough it will somehow happen automatically.

Another favorite pastime in playing this game of urban problems is to search for the one person who can provide a formula solution. Those who play this game are doomed to disappointment. No man alone can solve these culturally rooted problems. The way out of our crisis—if there is a way out— is through hard, painful work, first to understand the problems, then to try to devise reasonable solutions the people will accept, and then implement these solutions faithfully and fairly.

In a technological, physical, and economic sense we have been a nation of cities for at least the past 75 years. Yet, only in the 1960s have we entered ideologically and sociologically into the urban age. The crisis of our cities stems from a basic cultural lag in which our ideas, our attitudes, our values, and our institutional organizations are still rural-dominated in the midst of the tangible reality of complex city life.

Although I believe we are moving slowly in transition, American society remains caught in the crippling conflict of actually being a nation of burgeoning cities, while thinking and behaving in too many respects as if we were living nineteenth-century rural lives. Neither our ideology nor our sociology has yet meshed with our technological reality. Whenever this disparity occurs, and especially if it is extreme, serious problems arise. History attests that a society whose tools, whose machines, whose wealth and power exceed its ability to harness them creatively and constructively may well destroy itself.

Let me quickly enumerate some of the ways we are still geared to our rural past.

Politically, we have just recently moved in Michigan out of the era of rural legislative dominance. Most other states are still held in the political grip of their rural lawmakers, usually with disastrous results for cities.

Politically, too, we are still establishing villages, townships, and tiny cities. We have not yet matured to the point of developing a rational administrative structure to handle the vast regional problems of interurban areas. At the county level we are chained to a governmental structure that has not been altered for a hundred years, and which, as Wayne County dramatically illustrates, is archaic, unwieldy, administratively absurd, and unrepresentative, to boot.

Educationally, our public school system as presently organized and operated retains many rural traditions and practices. We keep a ten-month school calendar, which originated in order to permit farm children time off for summer work. We stick to a neighborhood-centered school pattern long after the remaining rural areas of the country have built consolidated schools and transport children great distances in order to give them better quality education. By and large, we still employ the dull, rote teaching methods of yesteryear, and yet we seem bewildered when our alert modern children are often plain bored by what and how we teach them.

Another rural carryover is our attitude towards land and our tax practices, which have not changed for several hundred years. Our reliance on the property tax in the large cities will be their ruination. As the property tax base has deteriorated due to age and obsolescence, and as we reduce that base by building additional public facilities, which do not generate taxes, the property tax yield seriously declines. A tax that served a land-based agricultural society has persisted unchanged into the present, and despite the lamentations of the logical and those on fixed incomes, there seems little prospect of a comprehensive, rational tax pattern that will permit stringent reduction of the property tax and increased reliance on a graduated statewide personal and corporate income tax.

Ideologically, we are still rural-oriented. Our outlook on problem solving continues to focus on the individual, despite the fact that our enormous urban population obviously precludes the one by one approach. The monumental problems of the massed urban millions require that the problem-solving approach be reevaluated. New concepts, new techniques, new attitudes are required.

Ideologically too, large numbers of our citizens hold narrow prejudices about racial, religious, nationality differences and seek to enforce segregation on various minorities. Such thinking is not merely rural; it is feudal in its origin. We have only begun the social revolution which will free us from this irrational limitation and this inefficient division. The size and geographic concentration of the vote for George Wallace in November will allow us to measure how far we have yet to go.

There are other ways too in which the rural perspective prevails in this age of the superhighway, the space missile, telestar and the computer, but these few instances I have noted should underscore the incompatibility of our outmoded ideas in our urban-industrial world. Perhaps this cultural lag is inevitable. But never before has it been so crucial to harmonize our ideas with the runaway growth of our cities and their amazing technology. The situation in our cities has become acute for all and impossible for many.

Even to begin the stupendous task of resolving the crisis of our cities and of our society requires first the will to do so. I am not convinced that most citizens want to pay the price it will cost to cure the crisis. Many of our citizens enjoy profit and prominence from the present pattern of things. As always, they will resist bitterly efforts to change the status quo. And make no mistake, the crisis of our cities will yield only to basic change of our society. We require a new America which we must build out of the resources available to us. We need a new perspective on our environment, on ourselves, and on our relationships with each other. We need a deep review of our values and on the commitments we base on these values. We need many fundamental modifications of our institutions and their agencies to make them function effectively in a world that changes fully every year. Unless we are willing to undertake radical changes of our current way of life, we had better not begin to address ourselves to the urban crisis. Solution of that crisis will cut deep into the nerve center of the society. There are no patchwork methods that can do more than postpone the crisis momentarily.

If we are truly committed to achieve the changes required to build a believable and viable new America, we shall also need three other things: plans and programs, leadership, and money.

Obviously, money is essential to cure the urban crisis. Much more money will be necessary than we have ever seriously considered for our cities. It will make no difference where the money comes from, whether federal, state, local, or private sources. Money is vital to help solve our problems. But, it must be quickly understood, money alone will not suffice. Mere money can only pay salaries and buy materials to build facilities. Money cannot create ideas, programs, plans, which are other required elements in the solution of the urban crisis. We desperately require bold, imaginative plans and carefully shaped programs to match, as well as the courage and the persistence to carry them out. Money alone cannot manufacture workable programs. Nor can money reorganize institutions or agencies, or alter attitudes and values.

Make no mistake: Money is indispensable to save the city. My point is simply that all the money in the federal treasury cannot build the new American society we must create. If, tomorrow, the Vietnam war ended and every major city were to receive a billion dollars, we would be unprepared to utilize it wisely. To be sure we could spend it, but we lack plans, programs, leadership, and sufficient manpower to use that much money effectively.

Despite the millions of dollars of federal grants, state aid, and local funds we have spent over the past twenty years for urban renewal, public housing, delinquency control, anti-poverty efforts, we have little tested evidence that all this money has made a significant impact in improving the lives of the mass of urban citizens. Federal grants should be made only where there is assurance that the money will be used fundamentally and not just superficially to resolve basic problems. Before any grants are made there should be specific evidence of built-in evaluation programs to test the worth of the project. One wonders how many programs have been started, tried, and then failed, only to be refunded because no one bothered to evaluate them. Too often, one suspects, federal grants are sought chiefly to show local citizens how alert and adept the local leadership is in persuading Washington to contribute to the city treasury. Only occasionally do meaningful programs follow receipt of such federal grants. If federal or state money is to be spent wisely and effectively in problem solving, it must be allocated to implement a comprehensive plan which local leadership develops and is committed to support to conclusion.

Speaking of local leadership emphasizes it as another element in the cure of the urban crisis. We must find and encourage intelligent and devoted leaders, both black and white, poor as well as prosperous. These leaders must possess commitment, compassion and competence, without which they will not be very successful. We shall have to help such leaders stand up and urge non-violence and political organization as the way of change. We shall have to help them build a strong, integrated peoples' power approach to resolving the problems of the city and of the society. Not only will we need high-level leadership, we will need, too, leadership at every echelon of the community. Too often leadership is expected to come exclusively from government. While government must contribute its share of leadership, so too must labor and industry and the church and education and the health and welfare agencies. No one has a corner on leadership, and so acute are our problems that constructive leadership from every source is welcome.

Unfortunately, otherwise enlightened and able business and labor executives shy away from personal participation in public affairs. Erroneously they view public affairs as enmeshed in politics, of which they want no part. Let me say clearly that public politics is as moral and effective as the majority of those who choose to participate in it. If honest, able men and women default on their civic responsibility, lesser men and women will assume public leadership and our urban problems will multiply and intensify.

If we are to assume a significant share of public leadership, we will have to consider such questions as I have tried to raise and we will have to take a forthright stand on them. Leadership can never be performed in comfort and convenience. The price of leadership is controversy and insistent concern. The challenge to all of us as individuals and organizations is to stand up boldly and answer the questions with creative programs and intelligent social action. Further, we should be directly involved at every level all over Michigan to accomplish specific goals. We must now attend to a comprehensive [model cities type]* approach that means:

We must end discrimination in employment and end segregation in housing and education.

We must close the gap between the affluent and the alienated, and thus build a more cohesive community.

We must broaden and deepen the anti-poverty effort for a real attack on the causes of poverty as well as to reach the unmotivated poor.

We must create a new definition of work and leisure consistent with our changing technology. Real jobs at fair wages must be made available to all who want to work.†

We must strengthen the public school system with sufficient, stable funds, better teachers and administrators, and more stimulating curricula.

We must assist the poor to organize into politically effective groups to permit them to voice their grievances and to have a say in affairs that affect them.

We must recognize social conflict as an expression of peoples' discontent, and act to remove the causes of that discontent.

---

*Editor's insertion.

†Editor's Note: A well-documented account of both the growing opportunities and the continuing lack of encouraging treatment of Negroes in a variety of corporate industrial settings is presented in Louis A. Ferman's *The Negro and Equal Employment Opportunities* (New York: Frederick A. Praeger, Inc., 1968).

We must involve voluntary health and welfare agencies in meaningful ways, and make the public agencies more effective. We must eliminate our present public assistance structure which is costly, bureaucratic, and undignified and replace it with some reasonable system of guaranteed annual income.

We must construct many more community facilities for people, including and especially housing of a wide range of costs, kinds, and sizes.

We must rethink and recast urban renewal and freeway construction to permit these programs to improve the social, financial, and housing circumstances of those they displace.

We must provide adequate hospital facilities for all, and low cost medical service for the poor and the chronically ill.

We must provide suitable recreational spaces and places to accommodate the growing number of people with more free time available.

We must develop additional inner and outer social controls to curb mounting crime, which affects all citizens regardless of race or income.

We must devise appropriate regional administrative structures that will permit reasonable, responsible regional planning, coordination, programming and implementation for mutual benefit.

We must replace the outmoded property tax with a statewide graduated income tax that will provide sufficient, stable income for municipalities, counties, and school districts.

We must motivate our youth to want to serve their community as the highest occupational commitment.

We must develop new incentives to encourage even better service from our public and private employees.

We must establish the means to train the vast additional manpower required to solve urban problems.

We must encourage churches, schools, social agencies, labor unions, business enterprises to review and to revise their respective programs and practices to become truly relevant to today's and tomorrow's fast-paced world.

All these things we must do swiftly and soundly if we are to resolve the crisis of our cities, which could become a catastrophe.

The challenge before us is not merely to save our cities. Barring nuclear disaster, I have little doubt cities will persist in some form or other. The central challenge concerns the quality of the urban life of the future. What will be its quality aesthetically, morally, interpersonally, politically? Is life in the city now the best we can achieve, or can we somehow transcend our current crisis and develop a better city that will be the nucleous of a new America?

Thus far the city has been merely a place for man to make his living, a substitute place for the farm, but without the benefits of the farm. For too many of its residents the city is still a place that is drab, dirty, destructive, demoralizing, divisive and difficult. The challenge before us is whether we can rise to meet our crisis, and by our collective will and effort make the city a complete place where men and women and children will delight to live, and where all of us will be enabled to live lives richer, more humane, more just. I believe we can meet this challenge. We must. At stake is nothing less than the future of man.

index